Mrs. Elizabeth Miller

They Met *God*

*A Number of Conversion Accounts and
Personal Testimonies of God's Presence and Leading
In the Lives of His Children*

Edited by

J. C. Wenger

Professor of Theology
Goshen College Biblical Seminary

HERALD PRESS
Scottdale, Pennsylvania

COPYRIGHT © 1964 BY HERALD PRESS, SCOTTDALE, PENNSYLVANIA
LIBRARY OF CONGRESS CATALOG CARD NUMBER: 64-15344
PRINTED IN UNITED STATES

Preface

One of the most moving experiences of my life is to hear students in my theology classes tell the story of how they met God. It seems clear that the path to Christian faith is not one of logic and philosophy, but rather one of repentance and faith. And this path to faith is most easily found when one is fortunate enough to have been reared by godly parents, a father and mother who know the Lord, and whose children sense the reality of their fellowship with Christ. In 1962 I asked a number of Christian believers to share with the reading public brief accounts of how they came to Christ, and what the Lord has been teaching them as they walk the way of faith and holiness. The result is this book. I hope that God may use it to make clear to many seekers that it is possible truly to know God through Jesus Christ, and to have fellowship with the Father and the Son in the Holy Spirit.

Every generation of Christians needs to learn afresh that Christianity is more than a system of thought, more than a list of ordinances and ceremonies, and more than an ethical system. Christianity is a living relation to God through a crucified and resurrected Mediator, the eternal Son of God who died as a sacrifice for the sins of mankind and was gloriously resurrected on the third day. This Christ is now exalted as Prince and Saviour at the right hand of God, all principalities and powers having been made subject to Him. This omnipotent Lord and Saviour has commissioned the church to make disciples of all the nations. But a verbal proclamation without inner spiritual transformation is empty words in the air. Men need to know that in the power of the Holy Spirit, God and Christ become real to the Christian believer. We can know God only because in His love He comes near, convicts us of sin, and draws us to Himself in love and acceptance.

Needless to say, the editor did not attempt to "correct" the theology which may have been held at various times by the writers of this book. Each author was free to tell his own story as he wished, and to draw his own conclusions. Neither the publisher nor the editor necessarily endorses every point of view expressed by the writers. Yet they do believe that the accounts of this volume are generally sound, stimulating, and edifying, for they attest vividly to the continuing work of God in human hearts today.

It is evident that the accounts of this book vary widely. Indeed, this is precisely what might have been anticipated. For God deals with each convert according to his psychological nature and temperamental constitution, and in relation to his home and environmental background. There is therefore no "standard" or "normal" conversion or Christian experience. Rather, the Christian life and experience of each believer is tailored by God to the unique needs of the individual. Christian experience is as varied in character as are the people who come to know God.

It is my hope and prayer that God may be pleased to use the simple testimonies of this book to draw many souls to Himself, and to encourage numerous Christians in the walk of faith. *Soli Deo Gloria!*

    Goshen College Biblical Seminary   J. C. WENGER
    Goshen, Indiana
    March 26, 1963.

Contents

1. A Soul Set Free, Anonymous — 7
2. Into Fullness of the Spirit, Myron S. Augsburger — 15
3. The Shining Threshold, Edna Beiler — 18
4. God in My Life, Helen Good Brenneman — 26
5. From Ambition to Contrition, Truman H. Brunk — 32
6. Obedient to the Call, John M. Drescher — 36
7. The Harnessed Fire, Paul Erb — 43
8. From Darkness to Light, Lorie C. Gooding — 47
9. Always a Christian, J. D. Graber — 52
10. Called to the North Woods, Linford D. Hackman — 57
11. Through Personal Surrender to God's Appointment, Lester T. Hershey — 64
12. Saved for a Purpose, Christmas C. Kauffman — 71
13. Saved and Led, Willard S. Krabill — 78
14. Called to Serve the Church, John E. Lapp — 83
15. From National Socialism to Christian Faith, Fred Linhart — 91
16. Called to International Witness, Nelson Litwiller — 96

17. My Conversion Experience, J. B. Martin — 102
18. The Lord Led Me, A. J. Metzler — 106
19. A Gradual Awakening, Ivan J. Miller — 113
20. What Christ Has Meant to Me, Paul Mininger — 119
21. Seeing an Accident as God's Mercy, Melvin Moyer — 122
22. From Rebellion to Discipleship, John R. Mumaw — 126
23. A Moralist's Pilgrimage, John S. Oyer — 130
24. Completely Changed, Ralph Palmer — 136
25. I Am a Debtor, Elaine Sommers Rich — 142
26. Taking God into Business, Al Richards — 145
27. God Creates a Pastor, Stanley D. Shantz — 149
28. Lifelong Learning from Christ, Elam W. Stauffer — 157
29. A Communist Converted, Ernesto Suárez — 163
30. Sought and Found, J. C. Wenger — 169
31. The Bible Was Nonsense to Me, Yorifumi Yaguchi — 176
32. Saved to Sing, Walter E. Yoder — 180
33. Forty Years at M.P.H., Ellrose D. Zook — 190

1
A Soul Set Free

(ANONYMOUS)

> "He brought me up also out of an horrible pit, out of the miry clay, and set my feet upon a rock, and established my goings.
>
> "And he hath put a new song in my mouth, even praise unto our God: many shall see it, and fear, and shall trust in the Lord."

God's intervention in one's life and the subsequent transformation are difficult, if not impossible, to communicate through pen and ink. This is because of the many facets of the new life in God which cannot be captured through verbalization alone. These facets include the gracious influence of God upon man, which is like an oasis to a desert traveler; the long-sought tranquillity, like the calm and peaceful sea after the waves have ceased to leap and roar uncontrollably; and an over-all awesomeness, as when viewing a countryside from a high bluff. Nevertheless, in spite of the difficulties of communication, I shall here undertake to tell briefly the story of God in my life. I must trust that the Spirit of God will make clear to the reader the glory of the heaven-sent life which I cannot adequately communicate in words.

I was born of poor, urban Negro parents in the year 1932, early in the depression. Our family lived on the second floor of a two-family apartment which was located in the rear of a three-story

---

For obvious reasons this writer prefers anonymity.

rooming house. The front of our apartment overlooked the back yard of a larger rooming house, and the back overlooked an alley. Directly across the street from the large rooming house was an enormous technical high school which took up the entire block. Many of the children of the neighborhood hoped someday to attend this school, or even just to be able to go in and look around. However, these were useless dreams, because that particular school was segregated, as indeed were all of the public schools of my city at that time. Opposite the high school was a small elementary school which the children of the neighborhood attended.

I do not have very clear memories of the depression period of my childhood. I do recall that my father secured a job with the WPA. I also remember that because of the economic stresses of the time our home was overcrowded with relatives. In addition to my father, my mother, my younger sister, who was two years younger than I, and myself, there also lived with us my father's mother, two aunts, and a cousin. Our apartment consisted of two bedrooms and a kitchen. To this day I cannot figure out where we all slept.

In spite of the severely crowded conditions of our home and the unfavorable circumstances in which I lived, I nevertheless have pleasant memories of those early years. We had enough food to eat, clothes to wear, and toys to play with. Sometime during those early years of my life my father began to drive a cab, and continued at this work until recent years. I remember my mother as a very desirable mother. She was a good cook and kept her house spick-and-span. She also kept my sister and me clean. The taste of *Lifebuoy* soap, and the feel of the hot water being poured over my head as she scrubbed me one evening, are still with me as a pleasant memory. She also took particular pleasure in dressing us. One outfit that I liked especially was a pair of short pants which were buttoned around the waist to the shirt. The shirt was made of some sort of silky material and had a ruffled collar that continued down the front.

My father was a playful type of man who liked to eat and to laugh. However, as I look back, I wonder if he had the requisite maturity for taking on the responsibilities of family life. I do not remember what the frictions were that led to the awful separation of my parents. Some of my relatives have said that it was Grandmother's fault, and others said that it was because my father ran around with other women. In any case, upon coming home from school one day, I asked where my mother was. "She is gone," I was told. She has been gone ever since. At that time I was about six years old. She did not go very far, just a few city blocks away, and ultimately to another marriage. But for us that was a very long way. On top of this, Dad soon left. Neither did he go very far, just far enough to be with another woman. But that, too, was for us a long, long way.

Our grandmother raised my sister and me. Even though my parents were separated from us, they did not totally shirk their parental responsibilities. Dad still provided for our financial support, and our mother always gave us gifts on our birthdays, and at Easter and Christmas. The gifts were given at a "family" dinner on Christmas to which we were always invited. During one particular Christmas dinner, I took the gift and went into the bathroom and cried. My weeping grew out of the deep disappointment in my mother, who failed to see that I wanted much more than a gift from her and a Christmas dinner. On other occasions during the summer we were sometimes invited to go to our mother's new house to spend several days. I always felt bad when I left my mother's nice clean home and neighborhood to return to the pigpen of an apartment in which I was being reared. By this time we had moved to a big rooming house, where we occupied a one-room niche on the third floor. My sister and I lived with my grandmother in this neighborhood until I was about sixteen years of age.

I remember the little elementary school down on the corner with mingled emotions. For me it involved anticipation, frustration, and exploitation. There was anticipation as I looked forward to the excitement of my first day in school. There was frustration when a kindergarten teacher made me stay after school to learn to fold a sheet of paper with perfect evenness. The exploitation came when my father sent a love-note by me to my second-grade teacher.

Because my grades were low in elementary school, I was sent to a trade school. During the summer following my graduation, my father purchased a small restaurant. All three of us worked there: Grandmother, my baby sister, and I. The neighborhood in which this business was located was even deeper in the slum area than our apartment was. Before school started that fall, we moved into this new neighborhood.

During my first year in high school my academic record had not improved. I had very little ambition to study. For this reason I was advised by the school administration to go to another city high school that fall. However, at this new school I still had no desire to study, and I did not long remain there as a student. In fact, after about two months, I was expelled. The cause for the expulsion was a cowardly assault that a friend and I made upon an honor student. I never returned to high school.

In this new neighborhood we were surrounded by people who were living a fast and wicked life. Thievery existed in many forms, prostitution, drug addiction, alcoholism, and gambling. As my father would not pay my sister and me any wages, we began to steal from his cash register. I stole enough to purchase a pair of expensive shoes.

The fatal morning came when a familiar person, somewhat older than I, came in and offered to give me something which would "round out my personality." At that time I was about seventeen years of age. I went with him a few doors up the street and there in a second-floor room I was introduced to my first "fix" of heroin. At this point I began a life of shame which lasted for more than seven years. If any reasons can be assigned for my beginning the use of dope, I suppose they might be that I gained attention from people whom I admired, and that the use of the drug made me feel significant, that is, I felt "hepped."

One of the awful aspects of drug addiction is that it is progressive in character. The victim begins by using a small quantity a few days each week, and this is increased to daily use and even a number of doses per day. The habit is also fearfully expensive. It therefore becomes necessary for one using heroin to become a "junkie," that is, one who sells dope. The addict becomes willing to sacrifice all his principles, and surrender all his powers, in order that he might reach his one goal, which is a greater reaction from the drug, more "smack." There is no halfheartedness on the part of a drug addict. He is completely enslaved to his way of life.

I too found it necessary to begin to sell dope. One summer evening I was picked up with several capsules in my possession. This was a federal offense and it resulted in a two-year sentence for me. The judge felt that I should be given the "cure," and therefore recommended that I be sent to the United States Public Service Hospital, Lexington, Kentucky. I began my sentence there, and after about two months was transferred, in handcuffs and light shackles, with many others, to a similar hospital at Fort Worth, Texas. After the completion of my term at Fort Worth, I returned home.

I must confess that after being "cured" for two years I nevertheless had only a shallow determination to leave dope alone. Strange as it may seem, in all the time that I used drugs I experienced physical sickness only once or twice. This was true even when the practice was continued daily for months upon end. In any case, my intention not to return to the use of dope was too feeble, and it was only a question of time until I returned to the needle.

This time my means of realizing sufficient income to purchase dope was stealing. Finally, the police warned me that it would be better for my welfare to leave the city in which I lived. I went to several other cities, in each of which I followed the same pattern of life, and the same consequences: drugs and jail. After being released from jail I returned home, and it was not long until I was involved with a group who were planning a burglary. I participated eagerly. We decided to rob a loan company in one of the shopping districts. It was our plan to take the safe to another location and crack it open. This plan was never fulfilled, for we were apprehended in the act of burglary. This time I was sentenced to four years in the penitentiary.

My experience there was one of great confinement, for I was kept in the maximum security division, and there was no possible way to escape. There was also no escape from restlessness, disillusionment, purposelessness, a feeling of insignificance, hostility, fears, and a miserable vagabond spirit. I saw no point, however, in making further trouble in the prison, and for the first eleven months I was successful in building a good prison record. After about a year, I began to think seriously of seeking some remedy for my need, but what that was I did not know.

As a child in Sunday school I had heard of the Bible and of Christ, and I now began to read the New Testament, and to carry it around in my pocket. The verse which appealed to me most was this: "Come unto me, all ye that labour and are heavy laden, and I will give you rest." I surely did need rest.

Another book which I read at this time was *Peace with God,* by Billy Graham. I finally told a friend that I intended to become a Christian. However, the other prisoners thought that I was joking and ridiculed me. Furthermore, my first resolutions were actually short-lived.

In my search for an unknown something for which I longed, I read a biography of Ralph Waldo Emerson. The book was so interesting, and so descriptive of my need, that I gathered two or three of my cellmates around a table, and we began to discuss what we thought it was that the author was saying. Besides speaking of the void and emptiness that is in man when he is without God, one idea of Emerson spoke to me more forcibly than any other. In essence, he said that man without God is like a ship in a harbor that has long sought for an outlet to the sea. It tries and tries until finally it finds an opening from the harbor, and then sails out into the infinite sea.

Some time during this period of intense contemplation, God intervened. He made me conscious of the fact that if I would release my will into the hands of this Jesus, of whom I had learned so long ago in Sunday school, He would lead me to life in all of its abundance. Since I was in such desperate need, and saw that I had nothing to lose, like a drowning man who reaches for anything to stay afloat, I was enabled by God's grace to surrender to Him even more completely than I had given myself to drug addiction.

There were four of us who sat around that table in that prison cell, reading from the same book. But how different the effect of the book was upon us! Although all four men had eyes, only one could see. Although each man had ears, only one of us was hearing. And although each man had a heart, only one was perceiving. It was God who called me.

The concern as to where I was to attend church after my release from prison did not bother me. I must confess, however, that I did think of the question. As a child I had been baptized in a Baptist church, but since that time my contact with that denomination had been very vague. A fellow prisoner told me of a group of people who visited the prison once a month. They were called Mennonites. This man knew the Mennonite pastor in my home city, and encouraged me to write him. This I did, and I received a visit from him prior to my release from prison.

In addition to my need for a church home after my release, I also lacked a place to eat and sleep. These needs were met by securing permission from my newly found Christian brother (the minister) to use one of the apartments above the church. It did not at that time occur to me what the Lord wanted me to do. That which I most enjoyed was to study the Bible and tell others of the great treasure of wealth which I had found in Christ. The ones to whom I most enjoyed witnessing were drug addicts.

My friend, the pastor, began to encourage me to attend a Mennonite school where he had been a student. I had no money, of course, but God, who had brought me this far in my Christian life, worked through my brothers in the faith to provide for me three months of study at the Bible school. I was also given a place to stay, and was fed. It was my intention to return to the same school the next year, but God had other plans for me. That summer I served as a counselor at a church camp. One evening after speaking to the group at the vesper service, the camp director put his arm about my shoulders and said: "Brother, the Lord has called you to preach. Would you go to college if you had the opportunity?" When I replied that I would be only too glad to go, he told me that his church sponsors a student at college each year and, since he was one of the advisers, he would see what could be done for me.

In this way God, in His great providence, has led me through four years of college. I am now in a Mennonite seminary. It is now obvious that He truly has "called me to preach." Not to obey

Him would be to bring upon myself that awful restlessness which I once knew. But God has not only provided me with a church home, and a place to eat and sleep; He has also given me brothers and sisters in Christ. These brothers and sisters are my fellow Christians with whom I have come in contact in many Mennonite churches, and elsewhere. In communion and fellowship with this family of faith I have regained that sense of being at home that was taken from me at such an early age. The church has been my salvation in many ways. Thus, the disadvantages that came from being born as a poor Negro during the depression, from being reared in a broken home, have been overcome through Jesus Christ and His people. Surely, He took me from the miry clay, and set my feet upon a rock.

2
Into Fullness of the Spirit

MYRON S. AUGSBURGER

It was my great privilege to be born into a Christian home in western Ohio. We were poor and knew the value of a nickel. I grew up on a diet of hard work. My dear parents were both committed Christians, and were deeply interested in the church and its program. We never asked the question in our home, "Are we going to church?" For it was taken for granted that we all would attend, each Sunday morning, each Sunday night, and usually each Wednesday night prayer meeting as well. My father was not a minister, but our home was open to visiting ministers, and there were a goodly number who made our home a stopping place in their travels from East to West, or vice versa. These visits made a deep impression upon me and upon my four brothers and my sisters. As children we grew up with the definite impression that our parents hoped that we would have more opportunity than they had had to make a contribution in the church.

By the time I was seven years of age I had already read through Egermeier's *Bible Story Book* eight times. Many of the Old Testament stories I could tell by memory. The Sunday school and summer Bible school programs had also stimulated my interest in memorizing Scripture. By the time I entered my teens, I had committed many passages to memory, and I had a regular pattern of daily Bible reading and prayer. Another influential factor in

---

Myron S. Augsburger is a theology teacher at Eastern Mennonite College, Harrisonburg, Virginia, and an active evangelist.

my Christian growth was the midweek Bible study for the young people which was conducted by our bishop, in which we were given weekly assignments for study.

My conversion came when I was twelve years of age. I recall having sat through a series of revival meetings. On the last evening a young man beside me leaned over during the invitation, and said that he wanted to go forward, and would do so if I accompanied him. I recall that I did not have any special urge to go, and let him go alone. It was almost two weeks later, after I had given some thought as to the meaning of the step which some of my friends had taken, that one day out by the barn I sensed that God was calling me to become a Christian. I went to the house and reported to my mother that I desired to become a Christian. She called our pastor on the telephone, and in a few minutes he and his wife came over, and we sat in the living room while he explained to me the way of salvation. I do not know what date this was, but I well remember the experience of kneeling with them in prayer and making my commitment to the Lord.

This was my conversion. It was the limited experience of a twelve-year-old, but it was a genuine experience. After a period of instruction I joined a group of others for baptism in a little stream on a Sunday afternoon. As the congregation stood on the bank and sang, the bishop led each of us applicants down into the stream where we kneeled, and he baptized us with water. The memory of that occasion will never leave me. It was a public demonstration of my vows to the Lord and His church, made in a simple but dramatic setting.

The years of my life from twelve to seventeen were typical of the years of development of most boys. Regular Sunday-school experience and the influence of my Christian home continued to stimulate my interest in spiritual growth. The Literary Society meetings of the youth group, and other engagements in the circle of Christian friends, contributed to maintain my spiritual conscience. In my high-school days the sharp line of distinction brought about between those of us who stood for Christian nonresistance, and the others who did not, was augmented by the atmosphere of the Second World War. No doubt this factor, as much as any other, limited the amount of involvement I was permitted to have in sports. At the same time I was becoming more aware of what an adult commitment to the lordship of Christ should mean. The contrast between the rather indifferent living that characterized my teens, and the claims of the lordship of Christ, created conviction in my soul. In a Sunday evening service I joined a dozen others in stepping to the front of the service in a dedication of my total life to the lordship of Christ. This was a major turning point in my life. From here on the matter of victorious living became a primary issue, and I began studying about the work of the Holy Spirit and the meaning of consecration.

The following winter it was my privilege to attend Ontario Mennonite Bible School, a time of study that opened a new field for me. The next fall I enrolled at Eastern Mennonite College. After graduating from the junior college program I stayed out a year. I was married in November, and my wife and I were planning to return to college a year later. However, during that winter we were asked to accept a pastorate in Sarasota, Florida. The remainder of my college and seminary work has been during, and in association with, my years in the ministry. One of the very significant things in my first year of college was a study I undertook on the work of the Holy Spirit. I wrote a paper entitled, "A Spirit-empowered Witness." During a series of revival meetings at college, a group of us shared in upper room prayer meetings, and it was there, waiting before God until 2:00 a.m., that I came to appropriate the fullness of the Spirit in a new way. From that day to this I have found that the secret of power is to keep one's life open to the work of the Holy Spirit. Truly a Christian is a Christ-indwelt person.

3
The Shining Threshold

EDNA BEILER

I used to be a skinny little girl with big eyes, a question-mark mind, and my nose everlastingly in a book. Although I was the eighth child in a family of nine, I lived in a secure inner world of my own, with growups and other children firmly fenced out. This seems strange, yet there were reasons for my rejection of reality.

I think I often caught nuances and undertones of feeling that were not intended for my ears, and which I often misinterpreted. Also, I was abnormally sensitive. People could shatter my happiness with a word or phrase. The inner world offered me security from change and intrusion, and a defense against painful adjustments.

In addition to this, as I grew into the teen years, I developed completely impossible standards of perfection for myself that drove me still further from reality. In real life I felt hopelessly inadequate. I was afraid to try anything without the most detailed instructions. In contrast, my imaginary world was perfect. The people in it behaved in predictable ways. This gave me the satisfaction of achieving, without the painful necessity of exerting myself.

You may wonder what I mean by an imaginary world. At first mine consisted of "pretend people" of all kinds. As I grew

---

Edna Beiler is Children's and Youth Editor, Information Services, Mennonite Board of Missions and Charities, Elkhart, Indiana, and the author of several books of stories.

older, it began to resemble the books I read; I simply extended my reading experience by thinking up further adventures involving the same characters. From this, it was an easy step to producing characters that came from my own imagination entirely.

I did not know it at the time, but my inner world was becoming a writer's world. I thought out the characters in loving detail. I formed my stories and the words so vividly that I could often see them on the page, although I never submitted myself to the discipline of actually writing them down.

Since a child has few inner resources with which to meet pain and misunderstanding, he must learn to cope with his problems as best he can. My solution was retreat and withdrawal. My inner world offered vicarious adventure without the fear of failure or rebuff. It was good preparation for me as a writer, but it did not prepare me for life itself.

I was baptized when I was about fourteen years old. At this distance, it is hard for me to give any accurate picture of my relationship with God at that time. As far as I know, I was a typical teen-ager, alternating between heights of joy and depths of despair. The spiritual life, for me, was turbulent, vivid, keen, but it was also characterized by underlying uncertainty. At times it threatened my inner world of daydreams, seeming to turn life into one vast dreary desert of drab respectability.

From the perspective of later years I can see that I developed an unfortunate misconception of the Trinity. God the Father seemed like a stern and unreasonable being, the originator of all the impossible standards of perfection I had set up for myself. On the other hand, God the Son was kind and loving. He was on my side, ready to convince the Father that He ought to be more lenient. Of God the Holy Spirit, I knew next to nothing.

Sometimes events that seem matter-of-fact bring a long train of changes in their wake. The Lord Himself must have guided my hand when I made those first halting efforts to put some of my dream world on paper. Here again, I was hindered by my perfectionist standards. I had steeped myself in the classics, and I knew that my own writing did not resemble them. Encouragement from others (among them A. Grace Wenger, my

English teacher, and editors like Paul Erb, Elizabeth Showalter, and C. F. Yake) finally helped me to see that in the world of literature there is room for the sparrow's chirp as well as the nightingale's trill.

It was then that the inner and the outer world began to merge into one. I was turning, in a sense, from dreams to achievement, from withdrawal to communication. The very sensitivity that had been a handicap and a weakness now became a source of strength.

Writing gave me a sense of fulfillment that I had never known before. I know that none of the hundreds of stories I wrote are deathless prose, but the writing itself, and the contact that it led to, caused the first tremor in my facade of isolation and individualism. The walls were not down, by any means; but they were beginning to crumble a little. The inner world (that I had thought of as a childish habit that should have been discarded long ago) was now entirely respectable. The outer world, that I had feared so much, suddenly became friendlier and less frightening.

I still had some very real problems, however. I had compartmentalized my life as a writer from my life as a person. As a writer I prayed much about my work, and trusted the Lord to direct me in it. I was happy and fairly sure of myself. I could even permit myself to make a mistake now and then! But I still felt that God demanded some kind of unachievable perfection from me as a person.

Also, the writer's world was still a safe inner world. It was certainly much healthier than my dream world, because it did touch the outer world at times, but I had never really overcome my basic distrust of people. I had no trouble with superficial contacts, but I was seriously handicapped in developing satisfying personal relationships on any deeper level.

I was introduced to God, the Holy Spirit, at a tent meeting where Evangelist George R. Brunk was preaching. I had been driven there by an aching inner emptiness and a fierce heart hunger. God answered many prayers for me through that contact. The Holy Spirit had always seemed vague and shadowy to me. He now became a Comforter in a very real sense.

But this did not heal the basic cleavage in my belief about the Trinity, nor did it rid me of my perfectionist standards. I, who was touchy and sensitive, should be able to accept anything from anyone without a murmur. I, who found changes and adjustments very difficult, should be able to make any change without question. I, who found human relationships as a whole unsatisfying and threatening, should be able to accept and love anyone, no matter how incompatible.

Furthermore, I should be able to do this without help from anyone else. The need to discuss problems with anyone represented failure to me. I even felt that the ideal Christian should be able to keep his spiritual life alive and vital without church attendance! In other words, I had set up a standard of my own that was not really Christian, and I was trying to live up to it.

Another important event in my adult life was a Voluntary Service assignment under the Mennonite Relief and Service Committee as a roving reporter. During this time, I spent from three to six weeks at various locations in order to write about them. I lived through bush hops (in small eight-passenger planes) in Alaska, a horseback trip to Coamo Arriba in Puerto Rico, and a revolution and an appendectomy in Cuba! I gained a sincere and lasting appreciation for the dedicated service of hard-working missionaries and volunteers. I appreciated working with staff members from the Voluntary Service office, and was happy for the opportunity to identify myself with such a creative and worth-while movement.

Yet, good as this experience was, it did precipitate a good many conflicts for me. Before, my aims had been fairly clear-cut. I wanted to be left alone to read and write, living in a secure little world of my own. Now, I no longer had this singleness of purpose. I had learned to appreciate friendship. I needed other people more. This seemed threatening to me, since I considered maturity and self-sufficiency as synonymous.

The day came when my inner world collapsed completely. Because I more or less equated my spiritual life with the world of imagination, the two were in danger of being swept away together.

Writing had given my life much of its meaning. When this

was gone, I felt hopelessly adrift. During those days I often said, "It's too bad that you can't stop living when your life is over!" I pause here to express my appreciation for the people who listened to my complaints, and stood by me during that difficult time. Although my VS assignment increased some of my basic conflicts, it also provided friends who could understand and help me work through some of them.

I came out of that experience with renewed commitment to God the Son—a renewed sense of His love as it was demonstrated by His death on the cross. Gradually I began to see that writing had been too much the center of my life, so that it had usurped the place which God Himself should have had. It was after this experience that the Bible became the living Word of God to me, with pages that were simply aflame with love and concern and compassion. I learned things from that experience that I could never have learned in any other way.

But I still struggled with my underlying problem of relationships with others. To me, a congregation was simply a group of people with failures and weaknesses of various kinds. How could this combined weakness really develop strength?

For a while I side-stepped my problem by an excursion into Christian mysticism that created for me (once more) a kind of inner world. However, the faithfulness of the Lord kept me from being satisfied with an experience that had little effect on my outward actions. I developed an underlying uneasiness—the Lord's warning that I was heading in the wrong direction.

By this time I had accepted an assignment as an editorial assistant at the Mission Board headquarters in Elkhart, Indiana. Although I enjoyed my work very much, my own ambivalence created real problems for me. I wanted friendship, but I could not seem to accept it. I was sometimes lonely, away from my family, yet the superficial contacts I had with others only increased my feeling of isolation.

I still externalized my problems. I could not see that my own childhood patterns of withdrawal and retreat were not adequate for an adult. I could not understand that maturity is not a straining for perfection, but an acceptance of yourself as you are, while looking to the Lord to transform you. Inner conflicts and tensions, which I myself often did not understand, made me touchy and difficult to work with. Eventually, as I withdrew more and more, my sense of isolation deepened. I began to feel as if I were isolated from the human race itself—a different kind of creature, strayed from another planet! I became abnormally aware of other people's reactions, and very much on the defensive about my own.

Since I was attending a fairly large church at that time, I felt that perhaps my problems would be less acute if I went to a smaller one. I had hoped that I could make this change quietly without too much comment. (Partly because I knew my friends would disapprove of this as a solution to my problems!) I was annoyed when something came up that made it imperative for me to discuss this with my pastor.

"Are you sure you aren't just running away from your problems?" he asked me gravely.

I had come to my decision after much suffering, and I resented being asked to reconsider it. The last thing I wanted to do was talk it over again with anyone. Yet, gradually some of the things that were said did penetrate my defenses.

Even yet I do not understand exactly what happened to me. Somehow the Lord helped me to see and admit some of my own faults. I had a realistic look at my own helplessness. Because someone was willing to pay the price of being honest with me, I finally began to see that the patterns of the past were not adequate for the present; that my striving for self-sufficiency was not really leading to maturity.

Yet, strange as this may seem, this honest appraisal of myself did not lead to despair (as I had feared), but to a joyful acceptance of God's deliverance. The straining after perfection gave way to an inner relief—a security that left me free to move out in worthwhile relationships with others. I actually forgot all about my feelings of isolation until one day I suddenly realized that they were gone! I began to recognize the fact that a congregation is not a combining of our weaknesses but a pooling of our strengths.

For me, this experience led to a new inner integration. Before, desires and fears pulled me in all directions. Now I could relax and focus on God's love. I no longer felt that I had to earn His approval by my superior conduct; I *knew* that I could never deserve His love. It was not until then that I really accepted God the Father, God the Son, and God the Holy Spirit, as a Trinity of love, yearning to develop my life into something quite different from that cold, flawless, and self-sufficient ideal of mine! The transformation which was begun then has become a process that still continues, sometimes baffling and painful, but always rewarding and full of surprises in spite of my own dullness in seeing the truths I need to learn, and my slowness in accepting those I do see.

I cannot condense the heartbreak and glory of this experience into a phrase, nor capture on cold dull paper that shattering and vibrant encounter with God. A miracle cannot be analyzed and developed into a formula. Yet, I must try to be as explicit as I can, else why tell this story at all?

In looking back, it seems to me that various vital factors were involved. These were: (1) Honest communication with another person, where I actually verbalized my own problems and admitted my own needs. I said what I really felt, not what I thought I ought to feel! (I do not say that this was easy, but it was worth while.) (2) An acceptance of the truth about myself that led to a realization of my own insufficiency. (3) A brokenness before God with a joyful acceptance of His provision for cleansing and victory.

These are not just conditions that I met once during a crisis and now can forget for ever after. Rather, they are underlying attitudes that I need to maintain constantly. As I do so, the joy of the Lord continues to free me from the old weight of fear and delusion. I can reach out and accept from others the fellowship and friendship that I need.

Jesus said, "Ye shall know the truth, and the truth shall make you free." He also said, "I am the way, the truth, and the life."

So I have found Him. He is not just a door that I step through and leave behind me, but a *way* under my feet. He is not some kind of abstract truth that terrifies and wounds, but a living truth that transforms. I learned to know Him, not by trying harder, but by trusting more; not by self-effort and self-sufficiency, but by being willing to accept from others; not by rationalizing my own shortcomings and limitations, but by accepting them as a challenge to His power to transform and make whole. For me, this encounter became the shining threshold that led to daily adventures in the Spirit. I know that the love that led me through the past, and enfolds me in the present, is more than sufficient for whatever the future may hold.

4
God in My Life

HELEN GOOD BRENNEMAN

I would not want to be guilty of plagiarism, accepting credit for that which is not my own. But the more I write, the more I know that there truly is nothing new under the sun. All that I am, all that I think, my every attitude and mannerism, I have received from someone else. I could not possibly tell my life story without hundreds of footnotes, giving credit to persons who have influenced me, who have helped me along the way, who have said just the right word at the right time.

And behind it all is the hand of God, arranging circumstances and leading in the choice of small but significant details. I see His guidance even in difficult circumstances. It is not hard to sing, "I thank Thee, too, that Thou hast made joy to abound." This song almost sings itself. But it takes God's loving faithfulness to bring one to the point where he is mature enough to sing,

> I thank Thee more that all our joy
>   Is touched with pain;
> That shadows fall on brightest hours,
>   That thorns remain—
> So that earth's bliss may be our guide,
>   And not our chain.
>   —Adelaide A. Proctor.

Ours was an unusual Mennonite community, in that we were

Helen Good Brenneman is the author of a number of books, the wife of a Christian minister, and the mother of four children, two sons and two daughters.

scattered over a large metropolitan area. My parents moved to Washington, D.C., when I was ten months old. At that time there were not many members of our persuasion in that area; thus, we met in homes and later in a rented hall. One of my early memories is seeing my father helping to build the little Cottage City Mennonite Church, which was my spiritual home during my youth.

Because ours was a small and intimate fellowship, we were much like a family. If someone should be absent from services, he was always missed. The children also were by necessity deeply involved in the life of the church. I can remember, for instance, joining some of the other young people in ringing doorbells and inviting children to our Sunday evening services. We would meet them on street corners and walk them to church. Sunday night after Sunday night I had the assignment of telling a continued story of *Pilgrim's Progress* with the aid of a flannelgraph. Always I would leave poor Pilgrim stuck in the mud or in the castle of Giant Despair, so that the children would come back the following Sunday to see what happened next!

I owe much to my home congregation for developing in us the conviction that a Christian is a witness. We grew up knowing that we as Christians were different, and that we had a message. I shall never forget an experience when I was fifteen. God spoke to me distinctly that I should enter into a conversation with an elderly man who sat each day in his yard across the street. Each day I told the Lord that I would be sure to speak to the old gentleman some other time. Suddenly, I watched the funeral director carry his body from the house. Up in my bedroom I cried tears of remorse. And I will always remember, as a teen-ager, seeing my younger brother in front of a tavern, pleading with an alcoholic friend who had earlier made a commitment to Christ.

I was ten when I accepted Christ in a tent revival meeting near our church. The Lord was very real to me, and I wanted to please Him. Whenever I see a young Christian with knit brow looking as though God has asked him to carry the burdens of the world on his shoulders, I can sympathize. For I remember how my family considered me chairman of their worry department. How literally I tried to please God, yet how often at night I sat at the foot of my parents' bed, sobbing out my worries and doubts. Always they were understanding, and I would be temporarily reassured.

During my teens my worrywart problems became more complex; I faced nagging doubts as to the very existence and goodness of God. Looking back, I see that my doubts were not so abnormal as I thought they were, and that they actually became steppingstones to a stronger faith in later years. I know now that I was grappling in private with problems which have bothered many more mature persons. I was not the atheist I feared I was.

Ours was a happy family, and although our church group was not large, we had good times. When we children became restless, Mother usually noticed, and planned a social. Progressive suppers, biking around the Tidal Basin, softball games, ice skating, wiener roasts, fishing on the Chesapeake Bay, and Christian service, such as distributing tracts, were the order of the day in our youth group. When our non-Christian friends asked, "What do you do, if you don't dance, go to movies, or play cards?" the question seemed almost absurd. And then two Civilian Public Service camps were placed in our area, which brought new personalities to our youth group.

In almost every testimony meeting someone will quote, "In all thy ways acknowledge him, and he shall direct thy paths" (Proverbs 3:6). And how true it is! A good spiritual exercise, which has helped me, is to look back over the years and see how little, odd-shaped pieces of my life fit together into my life and service today. For instance, I can still hear my father say, "Be sure to take typing in high school." (How would I ever have gotten along without it?) And then there was the school paper. That is a story in itself.

Every year during my middle teens I made a trek to Harrisonburg, Virginia, to Young People's Institute. For a young person in a small church group, this experience was a real treat. I well remember the puzzled look on the face of an elderly bishop in charge of a class on "Choosing a Vocation." For I had turned in the question, "Can a Christian girl be a newspaper reporter?" And I had in mind a regular reporter on a big Washington daily!

Ever since I was eleven years old, I had been writing for the junior page of the Sunday edition of the *Washington Star*. This meant a picture by-line, and prize of a dollar. In high school I had had a thorough course in journalism in my junior year, and with it the privilege of editing the school newspaper as a senior. Included in this assignment was attendance at a large inter-high-school press conference, and acquaintance with real, live reporters. I thought, "I have to be a newspaper reporter or die!" I cannot remember what the bishop answered beyond clearing his throat. But I never became a newspaper reporter. God had other things in mind for my life.

Following graduation from high school I worked for the United States Department of Agriculture for four years, in two periods, before and after one year at Eastern Mennonite College. This was a valuable period, learning to know and respect persons of many backgrounds and faiths. Working side by side with Jewish, Catholic, atheistic, Rosacrucian, and Protestant friends, I learned some lessons in witnessing to one's faith "where cross the crowded ways of life."

In 1946 I was engaged to Virgil Brenneman, who was in the relief-training camp near my home. A year after our engagement I was able to join him in Europe, traveling there with the first group of students from Mennonite and affiliated colleges to tour the Continent. Virgil had spent one year rebuilding homes on Walcheren Island in Southern Holland. We were united in marriage in civil and religious ceremonies at Amsterdam. During the following year we became acquainted with the refugees at Gronau, Germany, Mennonite brethren who had lost everything they possessed, even members of their families. But they had not lost their Christian faith. As we listened to their stories, and helped them find new homes, I felt that their story cried to be told. Later I shared their faith in the book, *But Not Forsaken*.

We returned from Germany to the Goshen College campus, where my husband studied for the ministry and I worked in the office of the late dean, Dr. Harold S. Bender. I learned much from this experience, one lasting lesson being that one can take time for people, even though he may be very busy in God's work. No interruption annoyed Dean Bender. Whether he was preparing to make a statement to Congress, or working against a deadline for a conference, he always took time for the student with a problem.

While we were in Goshen, our first child was born. We brought him to our little trailer when he was scarcely twenty-four hours old. Dr. Spock's ever-present *Baby and Child Care* was hastily consulted that first night, as worried Father checked on "Hiccups." During the weeks following, the wonder and joy of new motherhood was often marred by postnatal "blues," for which I was not prepared. The Lord did not seem very near.

When I could look at the experience more objectively, I wondered why I did not feel like reading the Bible during those hectic days. One day, as I was ironing, God said to me, "Why don't you gather those rich passages which could have been so meaningful to you, and which might have helped you following the baby's birth?" Thus, *Meditations for the New Mother* gradually took form.

Through the publishing of this book and other devotional material and through our ten years of pastoral ministry in two churches, I have experienced a truth which the Apostle Paul once pointed out. He said, "No temptation has overtaken you that is not common to man" (RSV). My need, my distress, my failings, and my triumphs are not peculiar to me. Human need is universal, and God's answer is for all. When I call to God in my distress, He answers that need. And this answer I must share. Thus, when I receive letters saying that something I have written is just what another needed, I can only answer (and it is not a trite phrase), "It is of the Lord; I have only passed on what has helped me."

I have known defeat and discouragement in my spiritual life, and I do not blame God, for it is not His fault. It was mine. Yet I believe that God "will be with thee thy troubles to bless, and sanctify to thee thy deepest distress" (George Keith). Every defeat, every problem, and every mistake can be turned to triumph if God is allowed to take over. Jesus said He did not come to condemn but to save. We, too, learn to accept others and to love them instead of condemning them, when we realize the grace of God in our own lives. As I said in the beginning of this testimony, there is nothing new under the sun. That which we most surely believe, we receive from many sources. From the experiences of my childhood and youth, I believe that every Christian must be a missionary, and must witness spontaneously in life and word. And God has taught me over the years that this is not accomplished by feverish activity but by a quiet and vital relationship with a Person. All that we do, in the teaching and training of our children, in teaching a Sunday-school class, in writing devotional materials, in witnessing to a neighbor, should be simply a sharing of a treasury of the heart, an overflowing of the spiritual cup.

I have quoted several lines of the hymn, "My God, I Thank Thee," by Adelaide A. Proctor. Now I would like to close with another verse, which is my experience of the present, and my hope for the future:

> I thank Thee, Lord, that here our souls,
>   Though amply blest,
> Can never find, although they seek,
>   A perfect rest—
> Nor ever shall, until they lean
>   On Jesus' breast.

5
From Ambition to Contrition

TRUMAN H. BRUNK

I was born on December 22, 1902, in McPherson, Kansas, to George R. and Katie Brunk. I was the second of nine children. Kind friends suggested that the name Lyman should be given to me, but my parents reasoned in this way: "Why not, instead of calling him Lyman, name him Truman?" and that is how I received my name.

I was highly favored by the prayers and dedication of my parents. They asked God before their children were born that He would let us die in infancy if He would by His foreknowledge know that any one of us would grow to maturity, only to miss the way, and be lost at last.

When I was yet a small boy, someone asked me if I wanted to be a preacher, like my father. My answer was, "I would rather *thet* [sit] down."

Because my father was engaged in church work extensively and because he was often absent from home, much responsibility for the farm work, and other duties, fell on my young shoulders. However, the first ten years of my life were filled with many joys, and as I look back to that carefree time, I see the highest peak of my happiness in my tenth year when I accepted Christ as my Saviour and Lord. I was baptized by my father, and became a member of the Warwick River Mennonite Church, Denbigh, Vir-

---

Truman H. Brunk is a bishop in the Virginia Mennonite Conference, the long-time moderator of that conference, and a leader in his denomination, the Mennonite Church.

ginia. The next ten years of my life were quite different. There were teen-age problems, conflicts arising within, and defeats in the Christian life which I had begun. There was a desire to do good, but the strength to follow through seemed absent.

There were also ambitions. The world and the ways of the world were attractive to me. I wanted to make a mark in the world, rather than to live a life yielded to God. My parents and others would tell me how they had prayed that my life would be dedicated to the Lord and His service, but my ears were deaf to their admonitions. I was very much touched when, a number of years after this, a friend and older brother in the church, Walter C. Grove, told me that he had felt burdened for me, and had prayed every day for years that I would be recovered from the snares into which I had come. Even after those struggling years were over, and I had served in the ministry in the church, this faithful brother continued his intercession. For this I shall always be most grateful.

The end of the second ten years found me out on my own, to find my way in the world. I packed up and went to Washington, D.C., for work. Great events were to take place in the coming years. On January 16, 1924, I was married to Ruth Smith, daughter of J. B. and Lena Smith of Elida, Ohio. This companionship and fellowship brought me much happiness. Life began to take on meaning again. I truly wanted our home to be Christian, and I began to feel God's claims on my life. I wanted the peace and joy which I had once known. These years, in short, brought me to the place where I was willing to repent, and to forsake every evil way. The fallow ground was finally broken up, and a new warmth of spirit came into my soul. Strange as it might seem, selfish ambition and the ways of the world became dim, and as the rebellion of earlier years disappeared, a willingness and even a deep desire to serve my Lord and Master filled my spirit.

In these years the Lord gave us several children. Our first baby died in infancy. This was a great disappointment to us, and we felt our loss keenly. However, we were blessed with three others: Evelyn, Truman, Jr., and Margaret; we also took Sandra, a foster child, into our home. Our children brought us a new purpose in life, and we consider them gifts from God. The blessings of home and loved ones have brought much comfort and strength for the strenuous years that have come to me. My home has been to me a haven of rest.

At the age of thirty-two I was ordained to the ministry for the Warwick River Church. I felt that this call had come from God, and it is to Him that I look for the strength and wisdom which I so much need. Whether at home or in distant fields of service, I have desired to serve faithfully and to walk with Him whose fellowship is life's richest experience.

The fourth and fifth decades brought more responsibilities, and more opportunities for service. These have required deeper dedication, and more patience and strength. The pressures of church responsibilities would have been too much for me apart from the upholding strength of a higher Power.

In this period another great sorrow and disappointment came in the passing of our beloved daughter Margaret. We would have been overwhelmed with this sorrow, had not God come to our rescue with the comfort and hope of a future reunion. I thank God that He gave us grace, and by an act of submission we gave her back to the One who had given her to us.

Looking back over my life I can say:

1. If I have accomplished anything in God's service, it is only by His grace and help.

2. The way has often been strenuous, and sometimes seemingly insurmountable, but always God has made a way through.

3. Though I am conscious of many failings, I am also confident that the Lord has led me step by step as I have committed myself to Him.

4. I have had many joys in His service.

During the years of my ministry, I have looked for and recognized special gifts in young men of our congregation. With what I believe was God's guidance, ten of these young men have been called to the ministry to serve in various places. Seeing the faithful and fruitful service of these young men has brought me profound joy.

Another rewarding experience has been my work in helping to establish churches on foreign soil, especially in Sicily and Jamaica. There is no greater satisfaction than to see the Gospel planted, grow, and spread, not only at home, but in the fields beyond. This has been a deep source of joy.

I have experienced answers to prayer, answers which have meant much to me. On one occasion when Lewis Martin and I were in Italy, we had made a special trip from Palermo, Sicily, to Naples, to make contact with a publishing company. After our arrival, we spent much time trying to locate this particular publishing house. We searched through telephone directories and sought information in every way that we could, but to no avail. In this large city it seemed like looking for a needle in a haystack. We were almost ready to give up and to return home without having fulfilled our mission.

Suddenly, as we were walking down the busy street, feeling rather discouraged, a stranger joined us and initiated a conversation. We told him of our concern. He said that he believed he could take us to a man who might be able to help us. We followed this stranger through the busy streets until we reached a certain door. Here we rapped, and there was an immediate response. A gentleman stood before us, with his coat already on, and an umbrella in his hand. On learning about what we wanted, he said, "I just came to the door to go to this particular place; follow me." We were at once conscious that here was a remarkable answer to our prayers.

Looking into the future:

1. The same God who has been my sufficiency in the past, will also be adequate for the period ahead. I do not fear the future.

2. As has aptly been said, "I do not know what the future holds, but I know the One who holds the future." None of us know what the next ten years will bring, nor even what a day may bring. We do know that time is short at best. Perhaps we may witness the glorious appearing of our Lord in our lifetime.

My personal testimony is that I thank God for every experience which He has brought to me, especially those which have drawn me closer to Him. My greatest desire is to be faithful to Him in all things, that I may finish my work with joy.

6
Obedient to the Call

JOHN M. DRESCHER

I met God! It was not because I was searching for Him. He was seeking me. It did not take long. The first time I saw myself a sinner, and Christ mighty to save, I stood to my feet as a symbol of my response to His loving call.

I met God in a personal way. He placed His hand of love and lordship on me, and somehow I knew I could trust the One who died for me.

I easily recall the time. The sermon was finished. In the quietness of the opening verse of the first invitation hymn the Holy Spirit spoke to me. I remember the time, not because I experienced a spectacular conversion, but because I saw a supernatural Saviour. And yet it was a spectacular conversion, since every conversion is that. Jesus, who died to save me, now as living Lord deserved all I was and hoped to be.

No one, as I remember, went over the salvation story further with me at the time. Simply trusting myself to my Father's love through the merits of Christ, I found peace, resting in His mercy and grace.

Upon my return home from that evangelistic service, held at the Millersville, Pennsylvania, Mennonite Church, I lay awake for some time. I shed tears in the darkness of my room. Spiritual light filled my heart and mind. I marveled that God's grace was suf-

---

John M. Drescher is a Christian minister, and the editor of the Mennonite Church organ, the *Gospel Herald*, Scottdale, Pennsylvania.

ficient to save me. I thanked God again and again for His love. I was a new creature in Christ through a new-birth experience.

I spent my boyhood days in Lancaster County, Pennsylvania, first near the town of Manheim, then Millersville, and then Mount Joy. Here I played, worked, and loved as other boys do. Here I faced the temptations and triumphs of youth. I failed often. I learned much of God's forgiving grace because I needed it so much. Also today I feel afresh those early thrills which followed victory in a ball game, in a job well done, and in spiritual living.

Strange as it may sound, even before my conversion I had a longing to serve God in the ministry. I attribute these early impressions to my parents, especially to my Grandfather Drescher. These held Christ, the church, and its ministry in high honor. I cannot remember my family ever speaking against the church or its leaders.

Grandfather was baptized in infancy as a Lutheran. Later in life he, with his family, united with the Evangelical United Brethren Church. Visiting in his home I heard glowing tributes paid to his pastor and the church. Every minister who had been a pastor at his church was honored by him. He loved to recall sermons, and valued his pastor's words. Early in life I received the impression that no one had a higher calling than God's servants, the preachers. God's work never appeared easy, but it did strike me as glorious.

What happened at church was important to Grandfather. Probably Grandfather was not the most faithful in attendance, because of a large family of twelve children, but I'm sure he was one of the most faithful in attention and interest.

Because of such love on the part of my family and my grandparents, my own love for good men and for the church grew. It should be no surprise that at the age of thirteen it was clear to me that God was calling me to prepare for the ministry. This consciousness had an impact on all my life and plans. My friends knew it. My classmates in high school and college considered my lifework to be the ministry.

However, I did not dare to voice my convictions too far. There were still those who felt that to say one is called to be a preacher of the Gospel is going too far, and is in itself a disqualification. But I began secretly to save money with care for college and seminary education. Throughout high school I disciplined myself in the light of this objective. In college I spent less than a dollar a year for luxuries such as ice cream and candy.

God always blessed me with many opportunities for work during the school years, and each summer while attending school. This proved a real blessing. I was able to finish four years of college, three years of seminary, and two summer sessions of school, free of debt. I received financial help in the amount of $5.00 during those seven years. I have praised God many, many times for His goodness in providing so abundantly for me.

God's faithfulness in leading His children is easily seen as we trace the course of the past. How He keeps our feet from falling! His mercies are manifold. He whispers to us, "This is the way, walk ye in it." God not only meets us in a salvation experience, but even better, He leads us in a loving companionship through life. He gives us the sustaining grace and strength to do His will. All glory belongs to Him!

I cannot remember a day of school life that I did not enjoy. God's help through my school days was real and known. In highschool life, with all its activities and pressures, I needed God's guidance. I failed Him many, many times; still He met my needs. He gave me courage to stand against activities which His Spirit showed me were inconsistent with the Christian life. He gave me grace and guidance in answering my high-school principal, who several times tried to turn my interest from preparing for the ministry to something more materially rewarding. The Lord filled my mouth with appropriate words in answer to an outstanding high-school teacher, who one day called me into his office and tried to persuade me to turn from the ministry and to enter another field of work, in which, as he put it, I could become successful and wealthy. I thank God for His greatness, and that He gloriously guided me through those times when Satan shrewdly tried to turn me aside from God's will.

Commencement time came. The speaker was a man who recently had run for governor of Pennsylvania. "Young people," he said, "you will never be happy until you are in the place God wants you to be." I had known this. But it struck me afresh. Again I rededicated myself to seek to be in the place where God wanted me to be. It was then that I determined that which I have needed to recall numerous times since: the place and type of service are incidental. It is God's will that is supreme, and God's will is always best. Time and again in my teens I prayed that I might know His will and might desire to follow it. Many times I prayed that God would count me worthy, in Christ, to be used in some small way in His "vineyard."

Study at Elizabethtown College was a rich experience. God certainly used Dr. Henry Bucher, then dean of the college, in helping me by his encouragement and kind guidance. His son Donald, one of the most intimate Christian friends I've ever had, died of a brain tumor while we were high-school sophomores. Dr. Bucher took me as his own son in many ways.

God allowed me to share extensively in the life of the college. As a freshman I was chosen vice-president of the class. As a sophomore I was elected president, and when the class chose to elect officers for the following year at the close of the sophomore year, I was again elected president.

I mention this because as I look back I realize that perhaps God was again testing my faithfulness to Him. Shortly after this, with the prospect of a good year in college, and with an athletic scholarship suggested for the junior year, I was confronted with another decision. Should I change schools? Perhaps if I wanted to be of service in my denomination, I should.

Yet Elizabethtown College was close, convenient, and not as costly as living away from home. To go to Eastern Mennonite College, Harrisonburg, Virginia, seemed contrary to good reason. I knew no one there. Some discouraged me even to think about it. I enjoyed Elizabethtown College. Yet I had the inner calling, which today I do not question at all was of God's Spirit. I decided to go to Eastern Mennonite.

School life there was a spiritual journey, and it included many spiritual milestones. The dedicated faculty, the spiritually oriented program, regardless of whether one was in a commerce class or in chapel, the Christian fellowship: all contributed vigorously to my spiritual life and experience. Here I saw all of life lived in a closeness to Christ and under His lordship, the like of which I had never known before. Not everyone was perfect, of course. But the spiritual atmosphere was predominant. I failed many times, but God and spiritual friends forgave, lifted, and encouraged.

The weekly witnessing program gave abundant opportunity to share Christ with others. Revival meetings and spiritual life services left a profound impact on my life. Coming to Eastern Mennonite College as a college junior I joined a class of dedicated young people. Seventeen out of the twenty-six men of that class are ministers today. Four of these classmates began what is today the *Mennonite Hour* broadcast. Others are serving effectively for Christ and the church in varied vocations around the world.

Betty Keener, my wife today, also was led to Eastern Mennonite College for her junior year. Although she had attended Millersville State Teacher's College, and later graduated from Millersville, our junior year was especially meaningful in that it was the year in which God brought us together, resulting in our marriage several years later. I thank God that He meets us in this important matter of choosing a life companion.

Going to Goshen College Biblical Seminary for my last year of seminary work was no less rewarding. Here, too, I found faculty, classes, and programs permeated with the presence of Christ's lordship and His Word. Outstanding in my mind during this year is the decision which Betty and I faced in March and April of 1954. Where did the Lord want us to serve in His church? I was asked to preach at the Crown Hill Mennonite Church, Rittman, Ohio, beginning in February. Approximately every two weeks we drove the 250 miles to preach. In the early spring we received a call from the congregation to become its minister. But there were other calls also. Other churches also needed ministers. The Eastern Mennonite Mission Board chairman, Henry F. Garber, pointed out two mission fields which were in urgent need of help. Six schools approached us to teach.

All of these calls came almost at the same time. Each opportunity seemed clearly a real need. It was then that we learned that the need is not necessarily the call of God. All of these were real needs. Of first importance was our commitment to the will of God. The place and type of service became incidental to this. Falling on our faces in utter surrender we received further direction from God. Never once did we doubt the Lord's leading to the Crown Hill Church, Rittman, Ohio. Nearly eight rich and wonderful years were spent there. It was glorious to sense the leading of God as He gave us abundant opportunities to serve. And yet how many times we failed Him! He, however, remained faithful. His people enriched our lives and enlarged our vision. The Lord taught us many lessons, and not once did He fail us.

The Lord needed to teach me a lesson in stewardship before I could really preach on this theme. He did this early in my ministry. Now the matter seems insignificant, but at that time it was very real. Our income was small in the pastorate, and of course we had little money left at the close of school. We lived carefully, and now and then put a few dollars aside as savings. One morning, after being out of school for perhaps a year, I decided that we had enough money to put $300 into a savings account, and still have a few dollars left in our checking account. Later that day while in prayer the Lord spoke clearly. If we had $300 to put into savings, could we not give it to His work instead? We knew that the Mission Board was in severe need of funds. Chills went up my back. How could we do that? It was about all we had. After a short struggle I told the Lord that if this is His desire, He should keep reminding me of it until the next day. I would then know that it was His will.

During the next hours I was reminded of many things. Our car was fourteen years old. We felt we needed new clothes. Our first child had just arrived. We would like to purchase a camera. The Lord kept reminding me also of the needs of the world and of the church. The next morning I shared with Betty what had happened. She immediately replied that she felt the same way. What seemed at first to be one of the hardest things I was ever called upon to do suddenly became one of the easiest things I had ever done. Where at first I cried, "Lord, you always ask me to do such hard things," now I found a delight in doing it. This has been our experience over and over again. He asks us to give up nothing but that He gives us something better. I went to the local bank and drew from it the largest amount of money I had ever drawn from a bank at one time. It never got into savings. Rather, we had the privilege of praying that God might use it for His glory in His great and eternal work. It was but a small thing, yet God used it at a crucial time to teach us an important lesson.

Now God has led us to Scottdale, Pennsylvania, to share in another aspect of His program. I had always thought that should God lead anywhere except the pastorate it would be into teaching. I had found real enjoyment in my teaching experience at Eastern Mennonite College in the last few years of my study there. The invitation to accept the editorship of the *Gospel Herald* was heart-searching and humbling. At first I had many arguments as to why I could not possibly accept. But Betty seemed to sense from the first invitation that the Lord might be leading us in this direction. He has so led. We have the assurance that we are in His will, and this is precious. Each experience such as this is just another opportunity of meeting Him in a new, enriching way. Today I thank God for His saving grace. I praise Him for His sustaining power. I am grateful for His guiding hand. My heart overflows when I look back over the years during which He has allowed me to serve. How providentially He has led! How kind His mercies are! It is a joy and a privilege to serve Him.

I thank God that He met me and I met Him. It is my desire to introduce such a Friend to others who have not as yet met Him, whom to know is life eternal.

7
The Harnessed Fire

PAULERB

Of my conversion experience I have no doubt. God did meet me and laid His arresting hand upon me. He did convict me and lead me to the foot of the cross. He did give me assurance of forgiveness. He did change and transform my character.

But all this has been a continuous process. I heard His convicting reproof again and again, and I still hear it. I repented often, in tears, and still find occasion to confess my sinfulness and my specific sins. My commitments of faith and consecration have been cumulative, and shall no doubt continue till the end of my walk on earth.

There are, of course, special days that stand out as red-letter days. There was the January night in 1906 when I publicly confessed Christ as my Saviour. J. E. Hartzler was holding a series of meetings at the Pennsylvania Church, my home congregation, near Hesston, Kansas. The Spirit had already moved upon my brother Allen and my sister Mabel to respond.

One night I said to my father, "Do you think the other boys would come if I would?" Already the gang-spirit had a fast hold on me, although I was only eleven, and I feared to act alone. I wanted the other boys—John Zook, Harvey Zook, Silas Horst, Earl Buckwalter—on my side, whichever it was to be.

The next evening the sermon was on the prodigal son. I was

Paul Erb has given many decades of his life to teaching at two Christian colleges, Hesston and Goshen, to serving as editor of the organ of the Mennonite Church, the *Gospel Herald*, and to the ministry of the Gospel.

deeply convicted, and before the sermon was finished I knew that this was the time for my decision, regardless of what the other boys would do. When the invitation hymn was sung—"Just as I Am," which remains for me today the outstanding song for inviting sinners to Christ—I walked to the front of the church and took the evangelist's hand. Then I sat on the front bench and sobbed my way to the Saviour.

Incidentally, the other boys did come.

The next day, a Saturday, we shelled corn, and as I worked the grain back into the corners of the wagon box, I was constantly and preciously aware that now I belonged to Christ.

But there had been antecedents. There was the day when I had fallen into one of my temper tantrums, and my father, instead of taking me to the back porch for a whipping, as he had often done before, led me, without any whipping instrument in his hand, toward the parlor, the front room that was reserved for special occasions. There he talked with me, kindly, and deeply affected. He told me how my temper would spoil my life, because no one would like me. Then we knelt and he prayed for me. In the parlor that day I saw clearly that there was a power of evil in my nature that I couldn't manage. I saw that I needed God.

And there was the day when the carnival was on Main Street in Newton, Kansas, where I went to school. I wanted money to take some of the rides. But my parents did not think the atmosphere of a carnival was a good thing for their son. In my anger I vowed to myself that I would never be a Mennonite. I might be a Christian someday, but I would hunt a church that offered an easier way than the restrictions of the Mennonites.

But I deeply respected the religion of my parents. Family worship, carefully observed every morning before breakfast—even when the threshers were there—made a deep impression on me. I shall never forget my mother's frequent prayer that we might in heaven be "an unbroken family."

Therefore when once I had decided to be a Christian, there was no question at all but that I should join my parents' church. I was baptized by my father in the largest class—forty-five—ever to be taken into the Pennsylvania Church.

Assurance that my sins were forgiven and that I had peace with God became clear from the reading of a tract. Preacher D. D. Zook handed it to me after church shortly after I was baptized. It told the story of the Passover. It showed that the Israelites were safe from the destroying angel, not because they felt safe, but because the blood had been applied to the door. Then I understood for the first time that salvation is by obedient faith, and is not a matter of subjective feeling.

And then there was the night when I looked up to the stars and suddenly realized that my old fear of God was gone. The guilt which had stood between me and God was there no more. I had peace with God through my Lord Jesus Christ!

But there were troubles and problems too. The Spirit reminded me of dishonest words and deeds. I had to pay a confectionery one cent for a pilfered "penny-grab." I had to pay two grocery stores for candy I had helped myself to when no one was looking. I had to tell Mother about forbidden gingersnaps I had taken from the box upstairs. I confessed to Uncle Mose that I had lied to him, and to my father that I had sassed him. All this makes me wonder about people who say they have never made any restitution.

I had the common difficulties of the stormy teens. I had trouble in controlling my violent temper and in keeping my thoughts clean. There was a Sunday when I wouldn't go to church, for it was counsel meeting Sunday. I didn't want to tell a lie. I didn't see how I could profess peace with God, and yet I was ashamed to confess my failures. But I never turned my back on God. I wanted desperately to be a Christian, and I wanted to find a place of significant service in the church. I learned to know the unending mercy of God, and I loved Him for His patience with me. I gradually learned how the Spirit's power could harness the fire in my blood.

When I was a small boy, and people would ask what I wanted to be when I grew up, I would tell them I was going to be "a farmer and a preacher." But in my teens my love for reading had told me that I was no farmer. Now I wanted to be a preacher or a teacher. Mission study classes during my high-school years at

Hesston convinced me that the mission field was the place where God would use me. At that time at mission meetings it was common to call for volunteers for foreign mission work. My public volunteering one evening at Hesston College was simply the expression of a growing conviction and desire to serve the Mennonite Church somewhere.

The story of how my wife and I came to serve in the teaching field, first at Hesston and then at Goshen College, hardly belongs here. It was simply a matter of closed and open doors. But when in the early forties the call came to leave teaching to become an editor, there was a struggle. I do not think there was any hesitation in doing the will of God. It was rather a question: What is His will? It was not easy to decide between two good fields of service, and so for more than a year the argument went on in my mind. I really wanted to teach, but the persistent call to the *Gospel Herald* desk, and the habit which I had now developed of listening to the voice of the Lord through my brethren, finally tipped the balance in favor of Mennonite Publishing House at Scottdale, Pennsylvania. It is a decision I have never had cause to regret.

Yes, God met me, and has often had to wrestle with me, but I have found it sweet to walk with Him.

8
From Darkness to Light

LORIE C. GOODING

It is a difficult assignment to write about oneself. It is hard to keep an objective frame of mind. It is almost impossible to recall events in their entirety. One may remember events of childhood, but one's reaction to them is not childhood's reaction. We cannot regress or "un-grow"; and all our added growth, experience, and knowledge unavoidably exert their own pressures. Thus the very substance of memory is transmuted, and one may not recapture the quality of times passed.

Because one's background and childhood inevitably color one's reactions to certain phenomena, it is necessary to say a word about it. I would like to brush but lightly over an unhappy and largely unprofitable two decades. My mother died while I was very young. My sister, my brothers, and I were separated. After this I had no permanent home. I was a lonely child; my friends were my schoolteachers; my refuge my books. One cannot, of course, grow up in modern America and completely escape contact with religion. In high school I became interested in Greek and Roman mythology. Having had no experience of a really vital Christianity in my brief and casual encounter with the church (a bazaar, a card party, a penny supper), I concluded that it was another form of myth and superstition, and dismissed it from my thoughts.

I had married in my late teens, and in my mid-twenties was

Mrs. Lorie C. Gooding is a Christian wife and mother, living in Holmes County, Ohio. In 1962 Herald Press issued a book of her poems entitled, *Let There Be Music*.

the mother of three small daughters and two small sons. It was about this time that my carefully constructed philosophy began to break down. I would find myself in the depths of despair at the thought of the futility of life. I compared it to a sea, each individual a wave which, after traveling many miles from its conception, breaks against the rock Death, shatters, and is gone. I sometimes contemplated self-destruction, as I could see no meaning in life.

In the course of time we moved to Smithville, Ohio. There I found the first real Christian I had ever known. She became my friend. She had a radiant testimony for Christ, but it was not her testimony which intrigued me. It was the way she lived. Everything she did was somehow related to her relationship with her Lord. She wasn't obtrusive or intrusive about it; but it was there. After I had come to know her fairly well, she talked to me about Christ. I did not want to undermine her happy faith, but I tried to explain to her that I could not accept anything so scientifically unsound.

"Have you read the Bible?" asked Blanche. I admitted I had not, but I knew or supposed I knew the general import of it.

"You are not being fair," she said. "You should read it before you attempt to form an opinion of it."

If I had one point of pride which was a prop to my ego, it was that I was fair and unprejudiced in all things. This being so, I would read the Bible! I was fairly well acquainted with the Old Testament, but had never read the New Testament. (I know now what I did not know at that time; Blanche went home and prayed for my salvation, no doubt for hours.)

So I acquired a New Testament and sat down to read it. First I read it through, just as one would read any book. I sat up all night reading it. I was still reading it at breakfast next morning. When I finished, I read it again. It wasn't what I had expected at all. Here was no vague idealism, no sentimental sweetness-and-light story, accompanied by an impossible ethical code. Christ was no mythical figure veiled in imagery and darkness. This was real; this was searching; this was demanding. Christ was real, and Christ was imperative. "Come," He commanded. Who could disobey?

But, of course, it wasn't as simple as that. I had no choice whether I would believe it. If I see the sun rise in the morning, have I the liberty to deny that it is there? But how could I accept His conditions? They contradicted all that I had been taught, gave the lie to my agnosticism, set at nought my vaunted "Scientific education." More than that: they required some major adjustments in my thinking and in my living. They demanded something in restitution and restoration. They crushed.

Then I decided to be a secret believer. I tried to pray. "I'll believe all your Word; I'll keep your commandments where I can do it without revealing myself as a believer." But He would not have it so. I continued to be afraid, not only of the radical changes He would require in my own life, but of the changes that would be necessary in my relations with my family and friends. This last, I believed, would be the hardest to bear. (The only mistake I made about that was that I underestimated the opposition I would meet. It was worse than I had expected.) For three days I was the most miserable of all God's creatures. I couldn't eat, or sleep, or work, or rest. Then, being able to bear it no longer, I slipped away to the grassy banks of Salt Creek and there I *prayed* for the first time in my life. I do not remember the words of that prayer, or whether there were any words, but the attitude of my heart was something on this order: "I can't fight you any more. I don't want to fight you. I have denied and resisted you, but I will not again. So here I am; do as you will with me."

I had no idea what to expect. I knew only that whatever He did, it would be wholly right. If He would demand my life for my willful rebellion, I was prepared to admit the justice of it. But then—not suddenly, but with a growing awareness as I lay there with my face in the grass, prostrate (I don't know how or when I reached that position; I do remember kneeling)—I felt, or sensed, or was somehow made aware of His presence. *He was there!* There was no wild exultation, no great light, no loud voice. But never had I felt such contentment, such fulfillment, such purposiveness and meaning in life. Never had I known such an inward stillness, such absolute tranquillity.

The point of this lengthy account is that this was definitely not a merely subjective experience. I was not psychologically or religiously conditioned for such an experience. No one had explained to me the "way of salvation." I doubt that I would have found it lucid in my former frame of mind, even had anyone tried to explain salvation to me. But if ever a life was touched and changed by an objective Force, a Power outside itself, a Person, mine was that life, and that was the time. This experience, for which I then had no name, changed the course of my life as an earthquake changes the course of a river. For me, this has established for all time the validity of prayer as a communication with that which is outside natural law. I believed at that time that this Power was the Lord Jesus Christ, and nothing has occurred since then to cause me to revise that belief.

This also proves, for me, that the goodness and mercy of God are not bound to any form. Even though my inept prayer at that time lacked most of the "seven elements of true prayer" (praise, adoration, thanksgiving, petition, intercession), and contained to the full only two (desire and surrender), God mercifully met me and filled my need.

On the following Wednesday I went to the little church where Blanche attended. There I found a real fellowship of the Spirit, and in a few weeks I was baptized. This was not a "Holiness" church, and all of the ladies had "bobbed" hair. However, with the Word and the Spirit to instruct me, I soon decided to let my hair grow long. Although nothing was said about carnal pleasures, I began to find them distasteful. I encountered much opposition, both at home and in the church, because of my "fanaticism." I owe an everlasting debt of gratitude to my friend Blanche. And I am grateful to God for that church where I first found Christian fellowship and love.

But God was preparing me to find another fellowship in a church patterned more carefully after New Testament standards. I needed and I wanted a strong discipline. I had a positive *thirst* for the Word. I began to realize David's cry, "As the hart panteth after the water brooks, so panteth my soul after thee, O God."

And then in the providence of God, we moved again. There being no church near us, when some good folk invited us to go along with them to church, driving many miles out of their way to pick us up, we went with them to a Conservative Mennonite Church. Immediately I was at home!

This is a personal record. There would be much to say of the Lord's dealing with and through us; of the children's acceptance of the good life; of His goodness in graciously giving us through conversion several of those who were most violent in opposition; of healings; of enablings; of providences; of consolations; of teaching; of the blessing of the presence of the Spirit. There is much to praise Him for in His wonderful deliverances from sin, and from the power of sin; in His grace in showing us that we need not rely upon ourselves, that He will keep, even in the midst of the storm.

All has not been smooth sailing. But God has always been good to me. If He can use this account of His mercies toward one who is not worthy to speak His name, then the writing of it has been worth the prayer and the time and effort which have gone into it. Any first-person account is necessarily full of "I" and "me"; but then, it was I to whom He showed mercy and pardon that day. It was I for whom my Lord Jesus Christ died so long ago. And it was I to whom He directed His command and invitation, "Come unto me." It is only I who can tell how graciously He deals with me.

So this is the story, and I have tried to write it as truly as I can, dedicating it to the glory of our Lord Jesus, "who delivered us out of so great a death, and will deliver: on whom we have set our hope that he will also still deliver us" (II Corinthians 1:10, ASV). To Him be glory forever. Amen.

9
Always a Christian

J. D. GRABER

I do not recall the time when I was not a Christian. I believed in Christ, prayed, and consciously tried to be in the will of God from the time of my earliest recollection. Someone will surely ask whether I then was ever converted. I would give testimony that I was indeed, but that my conversion, as well as my early Christian development, was more like that of Timothy than of Paul.

The earliest religious influence I recall is Mother singing over our beds as she tucked us in. One of these little songs I have remembered in full through the years.

> Müde bin ich geh zur Ruh',
> Schliesse meine Augen zu.
> Vater, lass' die Augen dein
> Ueber meine Bette sein.
>
> Hab' ich Unrecht heut' getan,
> Sieh' es, lieber Gott, nicht an.
> Deine Gnad' und Christi Blut
> Macht ja allen Schaden gut.

(The essence of this little poem is that as a tired person I am going to my rest, and closing my eyes. The poem continues with

---

J. D. Graber is a Christian minister and missionary, currently General Secretary of the Mennonite Board of Missions and Charities, Elkhart, Indiana.

a prayer that the Father should let His eyes be over the bed, adds a request for forgiveness if one has done wrong that day, and closes with the assurance that the grace of God and the blood of Christ cleanse from all sin.) I can testify that this little song instilled trust in the heavenly Father, gave us a sense of peace and rest in Him as we fell asleep, and in the second stanza taught us a correct theology of salvation.

My spiritual experience is rooted in my home life, perhaps even more completely than I am aware. Mother was kind, gentle, and trusting. Father was strong, disciplined, and devout. Standards of Christian conduct were high, love and charity prevailed, and as someone else has written about our home, here it was always considered an honor to serve the church. I believe there is not even a near substitute in the best modern methods of Christian nurture that can match the effectiveness of a truly Christian home in developing Christian faith and character. These foundations are made in the home, and if the home fails the task, Christian education by other agencies becomes very difficult, and often impossible.

A week of Bible conference and evangelistic preaching was in progress at our home church. We naturally attended every session. About midway through the week, one evening as the invitation was given, I rather suddenly felt that I should openly confess Christ. So I simply stood and did so. This is why I said at the beginning that I do not recall the time when I was not a Christian. There was here nothing of the dramatic, no long hard stifling of conviction, and no final yielding accompanied by an emotional upheaval.

I was about thirteen years of age when I "stood for Christ." After we reached home that evening Father asked Mother in my presence, "Do you think Josie knew what he was doing when he stood in the meeting tonight?" As the question was really directed to me, I simply assured my parents that I did know what I was doing, and that I wanted from now on to be a Christian and a church member. This seemed to be a satisfactory answer, and no one ever raised the question again. I went through the instruction class with others of my age who were "joining church." The method of instruction consisted of going through the Eighteen Articles of Faith in the Dordrecht Confession. The class was instructed on the front benches of the church by our bishop, Sebastian Gerig, in the German language. We had, of course, all learned German because our "Primary Department Religious Education curriculum" had consisted of a German (secular) ABC book! This we had learned to read and practically memorized. As soon as we were able to read German, after a year or two with the ABC booklet, we graduated to the German Adult lesson quarterly. Many religious educationists are properly horrified at this poverty of teaching aids, and perhaps wonder how any good thing could thus come of "Nazareth."

There were also, I should say, the picture cards. I remember these from my earliest Sunday-school experiences. Once the teacher asked which one of the characters in the picture was an angel. One of the boys identified the angel. When asked how he knew that was an angel, he said, "It's got feathers." Again I repeat that it was not methods or materials that were the foundation of our Christian nurture. It was the atmosphere of the home, and the priceless heritage of Christian parents.

Was my open acceptance of Christ in the public meeting a genuine conversion experience? It did make a difference in my life. The very next morning I walked and ran the usual half-mile to school. As I neared the schoolhouse, I saw a familiar drama in progress. Carl, one of the big boys, was somehow the object of persecution by a group of younger boys. He could easily thrash any two or three of us, but he could not handle six or ten of us. Our strength lay in numbers. As I crossed the road to the school grounds, I saw Carl cowered up against the building, while the boys were firing clods of earth at him. I thrilled at the prospect, and promptly gathered my supply of ammunition from among the clods in the dirt road. But now something happened inside me. I suddenly recalled that I had stood in the meeting the evening before, and that I was now a Christian. Whereupon I dropped my supply of clods and entered the schoolhouse on the other side. This is really an insignificant incident, yet it illustrates the fact that I knew it did make a difference in my conduct when I became committed to Christ.

From the time of "joining church" at about thirteen years of age my Christian life has been one of more or less normal growth. I am not conscious of any serious crises or emotional upheavals. I had my share of rebellious feelings and frustrations during adolescence, but through and behind all these experiences was the constantly clear conviction that I would be a preacher and a missionary when I "grew up." Like many children growing up in Christian communities, I did my share of "preaching" from the top of the wood pile or to the livestock in the barn. As I went through the cornfield across the corner of the section [one square mile of land] to carry a quart of milk to Grandma's house one Sunday morning, I delivered the speech which I thought I would make the first Sunday when I was home on furlough from a foreign missionary term. This proves that a child's ambition to be a missionary on furlough is not a mere bit of humor! I think M. C. and Sarah Lapp had been at our church service that morning, on one of their early furloughs from India.

Father wanted us to have the opportunity of some education. He himself wanted to go to school in his youth, but that had proved impossible. We can be thankful that he was not permitted to leave home and study law, which is what he wanted to do at that time. In those days he could never have remained in the Amish Mennonite Church had he gone to school. So he, in a sense, tried to satisfy his desire for education through his children. We were farming, and farm duties were heavy. Yet we managed by sometimes entering high school late in the fall after the corn was picked, and sometimes making up the work when we dropped out early to put in the spring crop. Father paid the bills for our education, and we helped loyally with the farm work.

Always the purpose of education was clear: to better prepare for service in the church. On two occasions I was chided by members of the church for wasting my time and my father's money by going to school. Staying home and helping with the farm work made a lot more sense to these good people, who did not then have much vision beyond being respectable, self-supporting members of church and community. My defense usually was that God has given us some talents, often not many, but He does expect us to develop and use them for the extension of His kingdom, and that burying them in a napkin would be wrong.

During my last year of college at Goshen in 1925 there was a brief weighing of whether I should teach at a church school or go to India as a missionary. The decision was not really difficult, for there had been from childhood this sense of call to be a missionary. My wife and I were in the course of time duly appointed to serve in India, and we sailed out of New York harbor the day before Thanksgiving, 1925. Our experiences in India were pleasant and rewarding. There was a sense of peace in our hearts that we were in the Lord's will.

Spiritually the years in India were years of maturing. A new language or two; a new culture; new tasks; and, above all, new friends and Christian brothers and sisters—all these contributed to a growing and maturing experience. Especially do we owe a debt to our Indian friends. Here we learned to pray. From them we learned piety, faith, and devotion. In India we could see the materialism and the often crass worldliness of the church in the West (Occident) more clearly. Our lives were greatly enriched by our fellowship in the Gospel during these years of service in India.

And now the shadows lengthen. We are much more conscious of things left undone than we are of accomplishment. There is, however, a deep-settled peace, that wherein we did the Lord's will, that was success. Where we failed in this, that was failure. It is an honor and a joy to be privileged to serve Christ and His church.

10
Called to the North Woods

LINFORD D. HACKMAN

I was born December 21, 1906, on a 26-acre farm along the Cowpath Road near Souderton, Pennsylvania, within two miles of the original Hackman homestead. My parents were Joseph Wile Hackman and Katie Derstine Hackman. I was the oldest in a family of six children, the first grandson of my grandfather, Joseph Freed Hackman.

My grandparents on the Hackman side lived in the same house with us, and after Grandfather came home from work, I would spend some time with him. He was a stone mason, but was also interested in colonial history and in pioneer life. I remember sitting on my grandfather's lap while he showed me pictures in a history book. On top of the cupboard rested his double-barreled muzzle-loading shotgun, with its powder horn and squirrel bag. I can still smell the cedar "slivers" he used to get fire from the kitchen stove to light the kerosene lamp, and I can still see the "shadow pictures" alive on the whitewashed wall as he formed them with his hands from the light of the lamp.

My parents were very busy with the work on the farm, and also had an evening milk route in Souderton, except on Sundays. My father took a real interest in me and showed me what was wrong when my bow and arrow did not work. From my mother

---

Linford D. Hackman, originally of eastern Pennsylvania, has pioneered for Christ in establishing mission Sunday schools and churches, and is currently located at Carstairs, Alberta, where he serves as mission field superintendent for Alberta and Saskatchewan.

I got my first Christian nurture. She taught me to say the prayer, "Now I lay me down to sleep." My parents taught me about God, "the good man," and about Satan, "the bad man." My parents also gave me effective teaching on honesty, both by word and by the use of the razorstrop. My mother loved to sing, and my father always listened faithfully to the preaching of the Word.

I had a happy childhood. I enjoyed school. If I ever had an idol, it was a bicycle in the period before it was my pleasure to possess one. As a child I decided that I was going to be a trapper in the North woods, and that I was never going to marry! For a time in my childhood I attended movies once a week, but then I decided to quit and went to the woods with dog and gun instead. I was greatly attached to my Harley-Davidson motorcycle. Sermons referring to the end of the world caused me to be very uncomfortable. In the course of time my daydreams about going into the North country continued, but I began to think of having a girl with me for companionship. My thoughts at times turned toward becoming a cowboy or entering forestry. In school I studied until I completed grade eight, then worked on a farm and on a milk route. For a time I also took up work in a clothing factory, but this I did not like.

A very significant period in my life came in the fall of 1924. On October 6 of that year I became ill while at work in the factory. By Wednesday I was very sick, and was afraid that I would die. Thinking that my end was near, I felt that I wanted to be saved, and asked my parents for baptism. They, in turn, got in touch with the ministers of our congregation. So Bishop Abram G. Clemmer and Deacon Hiram Clemmer of the Franconia congregation came to my home to fulfill my request. I can still see Bishop Clemmer, with his hair parted in the middle, and Hiram Clemmer, with his long white beard. I do not remember a word that was said, but when Bishop Clemmer applied the water to my head I felt Jesus in my heart, warm and close. I had peace, and was ready for death.

My illness was scarlet fever, diphtheria, and mastoiditis. The pain was so severe at times that I screamed. Indeed my cries were so loud that neighbors on the next farm heard me. I had two operations, two weeks apart, performed on the kitchen table. I firmly believed that I was going to die and requested that the hymn, "Must I Go and Empty Handed?" be sung at my funeral. However, after thirteen weeks in bed I recovered. As a Christian, I was received as a member of the church at Franconia, but attended at nearby Souderton because my boy friends attended there, and also because the Franconia Church was closed for enlargement at that time. I ultimately became a member of the Souderton congregation. Now my interest was still in the North country, but more from a missionary angle.

About the time of my conversion one of my friends, Llewellyn Groff, also of Souderton, accompanied by one of his friends, went bear hunting in Potter County, with the rather naive plan of going on west and eventually doing some real hunting in India or China! One evening in the hunting camp, while cleaning their guns, one of the boys accidentally discharged his revolver. The bullet struck Llewellyn in the cheek and came out on the back of his neck. He was quite agitated and angry, for he expected to die within minutes. Rushing out into the night, he looked up and promised God: "If you save me, I'll serve you the rest of my life." Immediately he was filled with peace and joy. When he was taken to a hospital thirty miles away, the doctors were puzzled about several things: first, how he could be alive, and second, why he should feel so happy.

The outcome of this incident was that Llewellyn also became a member of the Souderton congregation. He is five days younger than I. We lived about two miles apart, but prior to this hardly knew each other. As we became better acquainted, I discovered that he too was interested in the outdoors and had been a good hunter and trapper. We were also interested in the church.

About this time I traded my motorcycle for a new 1925 Chevrolet automobile, a touring car, and in time began to keep company with Ada Alderfer Clemmens, daughter of Garett and Lizzie Alderfer Clemmens. She too was interested in the outdoors, but was perhaps at this point not so serious about the church because she had united with it as a result of having been asked to join, rather than having come through deep conviction.

One of the influential experiences of my life was the study of Daniel Kauffman's book, *Doctrines of the Bible,* taught by Elmer B. Moyer, minister in the Souderton congregation. Preacher Jacob M. Moyer, the other minister at Souderton, one time asked me to lead in prayer at the midweek Bible study—my first experience in this type of praying. Jacob had been my Sunday-school teacher when I was possibly twelve or thirteen, and I still remember how he challenged us by addressing us as young men and suggesting that we sit up straight. After I became a Christian, Elvin B. Souder was my Sunday-school teacher, and a very good one. Llewellyn Groff's teacher was Elias Nice, a man who was also deeply interested in young people. In course of time the superintendent asked the teachers to name substitutes. Elias chose Llewellyn, and Elvin chose me. I then suggested to Llewellyn that we meet on Thursday evenings to study the lesson so that we would be prepared if and when we were asked to teach.

This we did. Soon we began inviting other fellows to come and join us in this Bible study until we had a "gang meeting" of from eight to fifteen young Christians. The first part of the evening we studied the lesson and the remainder of the time we discussed topics of interest to us "around the world." A number of projects grew out of this group meeting, such as the distribution of *The Way* in Norristown, Pennsylvania, the practice of tithing, the giving of offerings to various projects, visitation work, the erection of a Gospel sign, and enthusiasm for missions.

During this time our churches sent used clothing to Canada for the Russian Mennonite immigrants. I put some tracts with my name and address in the pockets, which led to correspondence with Jacob Willems, Davidson, Saskatchewan. When Llewellyn and I took our brides, about nine months apart, we decided that for our wedding trip Ada and I would go to the Peace River country in Alberta, Canada, as missionaries to the new settlers moving there. I purchased a used 1927 Essex automobile, added a trunk on the back, tool boxes on the running board, and a stove rack on the front, and secured a tent, bedrolls, and cooking utensils, all with the Peace River country as the objective.

Ada and I were married on June 15, 1929, by Bishop Abram

G. Clemmer, who had baptized both of us, and two days later we started out on our journey.

We visited congregations, Indian reservations, and national forests. We located Mennonites along the way by the use of the *Mennonite Yearbook*. Wherever we stayed, we tried to be helpful and make as little extra work as possible, and a number of people gave us good-by with tears in their eyes. We visited the Willems family in Alberta for about a week, then called on Clarence J. Ramer at Duchess. After a visit at Tofield, Llewellyn and I went to Edmonton, where we met Raymond Thompson, a well-known writer and trapper, who encouraged us to go farther north. The great day came as we left Edmonton, following the "Peace River Highway." It started out as a concrete road, became gravel, then dirt, and finally nothing but a trail. Our wives thought we should turn back, but we replied that we were going to the Peace River country. A number of times we had to pay to have a team of horses pull our car. Much to our regret we did have to turn back. On our way home, we stopped at Carstairs, Alberta; Portland, Oregon; Sacramento, California; and then east to Souderton again. We had been gone twelve weeks and had covered twelve thousand miles.

Llewellyn and I then turned to mission work closer home. We began distributing *The Way* among the people of the Finland area. This led to the opening of the first rural mission in the Franconia Conference. After six years as superintendent at Rocky Ridge I resigned, feeling that the Lord was calling us elsewhere. It was a number of years, however, until we actually moved to Northern Minnesota—in 1939.

When I was converted, my conception of salvation was largely related to baptism and church membership, and the Lord graciously accepted me at that time. I was born again. However, there was one thing which I could not understand. Many of our hymns were written by non-Mennonites, yet they were so expressive of Christian joy and salvation. This puzzled me at the time, because the authors of these hymns did not, to my way of thinking, keep "the all things" of God's Word. When we lived in Roseau, Minnesota, we sometimes attended the Swedish Baptist church.

At once we knew that they too were saved people, but we could not understand how this could be when they did not hold to some of the doctrines which we thought were absolutely essential to Christianity. Finally, from Ephesians 2:8, 9, we came to see clearly the truth of salvation by grace through faith, purely as a gift of God, "not of works, lest any man should boast." We came to understand that salvation comes not from what we do, but from the One in whom we believe. This insight brought great deliverance and joy to us. It led us to recognize all true believers on Christ.

I was ordained to the ministry on October 24, 1944, in the Lake Region Mennonite Church, near Detroit Lakes, Minnesota, by Bishop Eli Hochstetler of Wolford, North Dakota, and Elmer Hershberger of Detroit Lakes, Minnesota. It was planned that we should devote our service to missions in Northern Minnesota. I must confess that in my childhood and youth I was never aware that God would sometime use me as a minister. The first hint that this might be the case was given by Clara Anderson, an old Negro member at Rocky Ridge in the Franconia Conference, who said, "Linford, you will be a preacher someday." For a number of years prior to my ordination I did desire to be a minister because I was actually preaching on occasion and greatly enjoying our Christian work in Minnesota. I still had a concern for the Peace River country, although I felt it was not important who should go there.

In July, 1944, I attended the Alberta-Saskatchewan Conference which was held at Tofield, then helped in winter Bible schools at Duchess. During this time I shared my interest with Bishop C. J. Ramer, moderator of the Alberta-Saskatchewan Conference. In the course of time I received a call to come and help open work in the Peace River country. The North Central Conference gave me a six-month release, only to extend the release for another six months, after which I was released permanently. We then moved to Carstairs, Alberta, which has been our home ever since.

My work as mission field superintendent is interesting, and I enjoy it very much, although I wish I were better qualified to counsel in many areas. Perhaps all I can do is listen to the problems of the workers with sympathy, and rejoice with them in the triumphs of faith.

I also had a concern for Christian work in Alaska, and as the result of a prayer meeting in Eastern Pennsylvania, in which I participated, Mahlon Stoltzfus and family located in that state. I have had the opportunity to visit Alaska twice. On these extended trips I have frequently flown a plane, since I took flying lessons in 1935 and secured a pilot's license, both in the United States and in Canada. In recent years, because of health difficulties, I no longer pilot a plane myself.

For years I have had a vision of having a mission in each province and territory of Canada, as well as in the state of Alaska, linking them all together by airplane and by short-wave radio. Perhaps the door will even open in Russia so that we can fly across Bering Strait to Siberia and carry on the witness of the Gospel all the way to Moscow. I realize that I have always been, and still am, somewhat visionary; but I am unable to carry out these visions as I would like to. However, I have already seen much evidence that the Lord brings these visions to pass, oftentimes through the ministry of others, and therein I rejoice.

I must also bear testimony to the wonderful companion whom God has given me for my work in the home and in the church. Oftentimes the way has seemed hard, because we lived by faith, and as far as earthly security is concerned, we had none. Yet the Lord has always provided.

I find my greatest confidence in the assurance of Christ, "I will build my church," and my joy in having a part in this building.

11
Through Personal Surrender to God's Appointment

LESTER T. HERSHEY

On November 28, 1912, I was born at Youngstown, Ohio, the son of T. K. Hershey and his wife, Mae Hertzler Hershey. My father was born and reared in Lancaster County, Pennsylvania, and my mother in Concord, Tennessee, in a small settlement of Mennonites who had moved there from Pennsylvania and Maryland. Father had the privilege of attending Mennonite services every other Sunday as a boy, and Sunday evenings he often attended a Methodist church near his home. This led to his four older brothers all uniting with the Methodist Church. Mother often attended the Baptist churches of her community. This had something to do with the larger view of Christendom which was handed down to me, for my parents had wide interests for their day. I always appreciated the way they loved all Christians, both Mennonite and non-Mennonite. From them I learned to fellowship with believers of all denominations. Mother still carries in her heart a warm spot for the Baptists, in particular.

My childhood was a happy one. Home life was godly; discipline was Biblical, neither loose nor harsh, and never unreasonable. I knew of no other life than that we should help others to know the Lord, our first duty. I always looked forward to the visits of other

---

Lester T. Hershey is a minister and missionary in Puerto Rico, secretary of the Puerto Rico Mennonite Conference, and pastor of the radio program, *Luz y Verdad* (Light and Truth).

missionaries, as well as ministers from other denominations. Going to church was "normal," and I do not remember trying to get out of going to any services, for I did not resent church attendance. As a family, we worked together to build the church, and this was central in our home life.

My parents were missionaries in Argentina when I was a boy. I well remember the missionary councils held in that land. At such times the children had lots of fun. These meetings were held annually, and we didn't see each other very often in between. One year we children decided to make some money at these missionary councils. Three of us older ones made ice cream and sold it to the adults. We cleared a considerable amount of cash!

Foreigners were few in that part of Argentina, and so any Canadian, American, or Englishman, even though he was not of our mission, was a welcome friend. Such a person was Mr. Hamilton, who owned a large cattle and hog ranch not far from Trenque Lauquen, where our home was located. My delight as a youth was the two summers which I spent vacationing on that ranch. We rode horses and rounded up hogs or cattle. With the Argentine Gauchos we rode and herded before daylight. At daybreak we would stop, and the cook would have our maté [tea] and bread ready for breakfast.

Furloughs were also delightful times, for we would again see our cousins, uncles, and aunts. I remember one furlough in particular. I did not always travel with Dad to his many assignments, but on several occasions I did. I always shrank from the many handshakes and embraces which the brethren gave to me as the son of T. K. Hershey. On one occasion, when I was somewhat older, my father was greeted with a kiss by a certain bishop. I was introduced as his son. This bishop shook my hand, held it for a moment, and then inquired of my father, "Is he a brother?" It was a most embarrassing moment for me, for I did not know what he was going to do. I learned that I was spared being "greeted," since I was not yet a baptized member of the church.

Evangelistic meetings were held in the church which we attended on one of our furloughs, and during those meetings I felt led to respond to the invitation which was given to accept Christ.

This was a severely plain church. As several persons filed to the anteroom after the service, to make known their decision to accept the Lord, I too walked down the aisle. However, I was not dressed like the other boys. I wore knickers, a lapel coat, and a small tie. I overheard the local bishop, whom I both knew and respected, ask the other minister, "Who is that English person coming down?" This made me feel like an outsider, something which I had never experienced until that moment, even though I had not been dressing like the others. Suddenly I turned and went out the back door of the church. I did not make any further move to become a Christian until I was back in Argentina. There I felt more at home, and had made up my mind that I would be baptized there.

I also remember having been appalled at what seemed to me to be a low level of moral life on the part of the boys with whom I associated when on furlough. Actually, their morals were not much lower than those which I had known in Argentina, but somehow I felt that I could excuse the Argentines, for they had not had Christian home training. But these North American boys had had such training. For me it was often a battle whether to go along with some of these unconverted boys, or to resist. The thought that I did not want to do anything that would bring reproach upon my father and mother kept me from following the example set by some of the members of the church in the homeland. One thing I did learn to do with ease. When a preacher in my opinion did not have much to offer, I could lay my head on the bench in front and sleep, or pretend to.

An example of the kind of situation which provoked serious problems in my mind is the following. I was thirteen years of age when I was approached by a boy a year older than myself: "Lester, you know the customs here in our church. I will soon be fifteen years of age, and it is expected that I 'join up.' But I do not feel as if anything has happened to me. However, if I don't join, my parents will think that I am awful, and the bishop, who is Mother's uncle, will ask the folks why I am resisting uniting with the church. What would you do if you were in my place?"

I remember answering him, "If I did not feel inside that I was converted, I would not unite with the church." I learned the following year, however, that he did join. Several years later, when I visited in that congregation, I was impressed with the indifference of that man toward Christ and the church.

I must give as my sincere testimony the fact that it was my godly parents, as well as those who were soundly converted to the Lord on the mission field, those godly and prayerful members of our church in Argentina, who contributed much toward keeping me "in love with the church" and toward my holding in high regard what the Gospel can do for people. Those converts in Argentina, who left off their sinful lives upon accepting the Gospel, revealed the meaning of being a new man in Christ. I did not fully sense this at the time, but now I can clearly see the great influence which the lives of those believers had upon me.

As to my conversion, for some time I had felt myself a sinner, and in need of a Saviour. Others always spoke of me as a good boy, and I felt that if I should make a public confession of my sins, I would be looked upon as not so good after all! I therefore put off making a public confession for at least a year, until I heard that particular message while in the States, and raised my hand. I felt that night that I had to get this out of my system, that I simply had to make the decision for Christ. I feel that I was sincere when I raised my hand to become a believer, but when I was considered "English" for the way I dressed, I was hurt, and I felt somewhat resentful. Later on I told my parents about this incident, and at that point I made up my mind to have nothing to do with the Mennonite Church in America, but to wait until I returned to Argentina. I actually made a public decision at a service in Argentina when my father gave the invitation. There was no particular sinful act which caused me to turn to the Lord. It was simply a combination of being taught that all of us are sinful creatures, having inherited a sinful nature from Adam, that we stand in need of forgiveness for our sins, as well as for the particular acts which are wrong. There was no particular struggle over giving up any individual sin. It was just a general awareness that I was a sinner and needed to get right with the Lord.

When I made my decision to become a Christian I went to the prayer room with several others, and prayer was made in general for all of us, as we confessed our sins in our hearts to the Lord. Of course, I had often heard the prayers of my mother and father at family devotions for my salvation. I used to feel quite miserable at those times. I remember feeling that I hated to attend family devotions, for I was sure that they would again mention my name to the Lord as one in need of salvation. This was the Holy Spirit convicting me of my need of Christ.

I was prepared for baptism by attending a class of instruction for converts. We studied outlines which my father had prepared in booklet form, and which were used by all of our congregations in Argentina. It was in the year 1928 when I was baptized by my father, who was pastor of the congregation in Trenque Lauquen.

Christian assurance was not a problem to me. When I accepted Christ, I felt sure that He had saved me, because I had done exactly what the Word of God said that I should do: I had received Christ as my Saviour, and I believed that He had saved me. But in later years, as I served in various capacities in the church, the idea did sometimes come to me that perhaps I was not really saved. When confronted by certain temptations, the thought came to me repeatedly: "If I am saved, why am I tempted in this way?" I cannot give the date and hour when I received the assurance of salvation, but I do know that all of a sudden it dawned upon me that I now had this assurance. I believe that Christian assurance came to me from the study of the Word of God in preparation for sermons and in my devotions. My sense of Christian assurance is enhanced as, on every occasion when I need God's grace, and ask for a fresh infilling of His Spirit, God gives it to me.

I cannot point to any one man in the church, or on the mission field, who has been of most help to me in my spiritual growth. I have learned from many Christians, of course. I think that my spiritual growth has come about through personal fellowship with my Lord and through His Word. A new convert always stimulates me, as I see the change which is made in his life, his change of heart, and the new creation which he becomes in Christ. It gives me a spiritual "boost" every time.

It is now easier for me to go up to a man and speak to him about his need of a Saviour than it once was. Somehow the Lord seems to give me the grace to reason with the man. He brings Scripture references to my mind, and supplies the tact which I do not have of myself. Likewise, evangelistic preaching has become easier for me than it once was. Illustrations come to mind as I proclaim the Gospel, vivid conversions are easier to narrate, my feeling of responsibility for the lost has increased, and I have a strong sense of urgency to help people. It is also a delightful experience to give financially to the support of the Lord's work. Quite a few years ago my wife Alta and I decided to give more than the tenth. In almost every year since that time, our giving has amounted to at least twenty per cent of our income. We love to give, for we are doing it for our Lord.

I must also state that I have experienced a number of spiritual crises or "awakenings" since my conversion and baptism. I do not particularly like to speak about these experiences. They are so sacred as a part of my personal experience with the Lord, that I have not previously revealed any of them to anyone: I remember one in particular. I was depressed from overwork and was sorely tempted. I am sure that my family could tell that I was under tension of some sort. Prayer to me in those days was my very food. I prayed much, and searched the Word for the answer I needed. I must say that God taught me much through those days of testing. My confidence in His answer to my petition was solid. I knew that He would come through with His help, and that I would in the end be better qualified to serve Him. I knew also that He meant to teach me patience, resignation to His will, and dependence upon Him in a greater way than I had practiced it in the past. I can well remember the occasion when I felt His kind hand upon me, after I had passed the crisis, and when I had complete assurance that He had answered my petition. Then my fellowship with Him was keener and deeper than before. I felt that even my body was touched by Him, that I had more strength to serve Him, that my mind was clearer, and that I was renewed both in strength and in ability. It seemed to me that a cool wave went over me as I knelt. Tears of gratitude flowed down my cheeks. I was alone at that early hour, and I could do nothing other than cry out, "*Hallelujah!* Thou hast done it! I am renewed! Praise God!"

I simply remained there upon my knees, basking in that renewed fellowship and spiritual strength, not wanting the experience to come to an end. Truly God is good to me every day.

What has God been trying to teach me in the recent past? The answer is—patience. I need to learn to show more regard for others, even when I cannot see their point of view, or if I do not appreciate it. I have had many struggles on this matter of patience.

I should also like to testify to how the Lord has taught me over a period of years to depend upon Him for direction, and to be willing to fit into His plan, rather than to make my own. Indeed this is the reason I am in Puerto Rico. The Lord led me to give up what had been my ambition for a number of years of my youth (namely, to become an osteopathic physician) in order to prepare for the ministry. Likewise, He led me away from the field of printing to a radio ministry which now covers a large section of the Spanish-speaking world. But even if I did give up medicine in favor of a Bible major, with the idea of seminary later, there were still other hurdles to be overcome. Relief work in Spain and Europe was cut short because I needed to return to the States to prepare further for work in Argentina. After seven years in the Spanish field in Chicago, this too was curtailed, since I had once more applied to go to Argentina. This had gone as far as having purchased a ticket on a vessel, the securing of a passport for myself and family, and the appointment of the Mission Board to go to Argentina. But the government of that land, then ruled by Perón, could not locate my identification card, which was then necessary to re-enter Argentina. Consequently, the Mission Board asked us to go to Puerto Rico for a two-year period, after which they planned to send us to Argentina. It took us several months to come to the place where we consented to this change of plans. However, after two terms of service in Puerto Rico, we have returned here. I am now entirely satisfied that this is where the Lord wanted me all the time. He took me through relief work in Spain, the Spanish pastorate in Chicago, several conference positions in Illinois, and even a bit of radio experience, as well as Christian journalism and Bible school teaching, to prepare me for the type of ministry in which I am now engaged. I praise Him for the way He has led.

12
Saved for a Purpose

CHRISTMAS CAROL KAUFFMAN

Mine was a delightfully happy childhood. Mother was an eleven-term Lancaster County, Pennsylvania, schoolteacher, and Papa was a sweet tenor, a sheet-metal contractor. Although they were not wealthy, they possessed the best things in life, which dollars cannot supply. That I was wanted, loved, appreciated, never was in question. I enjoyed a blessed sense of security and we also had enough of the things which money can buy.

Fashionable Selena Belle Wade and ambitious twenty-one-year-old Abraham Miller took daring and drastic steps when they became early converts of the pioneer Mennonite evangelist, John S. Coffman. Against opposition they embraced the faith which gave them peace, and eight years later established a family-altar home in Elkhart, Indiana, within a stone's throw of Evangelist Coffman's home.

From my earliest childhood until the day I left home I heard my father mention my name daily to God. Before I could frame a sentence, I was taught table and bedtime prayers, short Scripture verses, and simple sacred songs. It is small wonder that before I started to school God was to me a living, real, loving, ever-present, ever-hearing person, who, though invisible, lived in our home and accompanied each of us wherever we went. I talked to God as my parents did. He heard me. Of that I was confident.

Christmas Carol Kauffman is a writer of Christian fiction, as well as a Christian wife and mother. Her home is in Elkhart, Indiana.

When I was seven, my sister Esther, aged three, and I got inflammatory rheumatism, complicated by typhoid fever to the point of delirium. We heard many prayers go up for us. Instead of being healed Esther contracted diphtheria and polio, which meant that Nellie, aged twelve, and I were in long quarantine upstairs. Papa delivered our meals by ladder at the window. "Esther is drastically ill; we must keep praying." I felt a definite responsibility to help pray, but Papa had read from the Bible that if anyone has sin in his heart, God will not hear. I wanted God to hear me, but I had deliberately disobeyed about a certain thing. It bothered me. One night I confessed this to God, and in simple faith-believing words asked Him to let me see a real angel so that I would know I was forgiven, and be assured that Esther would get well. Soon an angel came to the window and smiled at me. This experience alone would take many pages to tell, for the following night three angels came, and the third night several more. I called Papa each time; he was moved to tears. Over half a century has passed, but the incident is still real to both Papa and me, and it has had its refining influence on me ever since.

Never once did I feel that being born into a Christian home automatically made me a Christian. Nor being told I came as an answer to prayer, and that my birth restored Mother to health after five years of semi-invalidism. Nor yet that I was dedicated to God before and after conception. This has, however, had a tremendous impact on my life to this moment.

At ten I was fully aware of my lost condition. I knew when I stood up to confess Christ that I needed to say, "All we like sheep," and to receive Christ's blood for cleansing. Most of this awareness came to me gradually while listening to Papa read and pray each morning. The instant I took my stand I knew I was forgiven, cleansed, and saved. Papa was the first to fold me in his arms and kiss me after the benediction. "This makes us very happy, Carol," he whispered. "God brought you into the world for a definite purpose." For days my feet scarcely touched the ground. I felt free, birdlike, light, and happy. No fear. No condemnation. No doubt.

I attended three instruction meetings for baptism, but the impression I got was that to be a good Christian meant *not* doing the many bad things the people of the world do. I would have felt like a hemmed-in, tied-back applicant had it not been for the positive, the pleasing, the many "happy can" doings, the why's and the why nots for a Christian, that my own mother explained. She knew!

For the next seven consecutive years Mother was my Sunday-school teacher. Every Bible story came alive when she spoke. We learned. We studied willingly. We memorized Scripture with pleasure. She loved her class. Mother was not a public speaker, but many of the deeper meanings of the Word she got across to her class may never have been grasped elsewhere. I learned the joys of personal work from her. Whenever a new family moved into the neighborhood, she was the first to call and invite them to church. She was loaded with ideas for winning new friends. She had a passion for the lost, the lonely, the neglected.

My growing years were far from dull and drab. Because I was the tomboy of the four daughters, I got to accompany Papa on occasional business trips. We also painted the garage, mowed the yard, trimmed the hedge together. He got me a red pedal automobile with a horn and a rumble seat. After that a bicycle. Not a game, a toy, a box house, or a book did I wish for that he didn't get in due time. Papa was positive, but wonderful. Once he took me to a theater to see the birth of Christ. Once he took Nellie and me to a circus. On the way home he explained why we would not go again. We never begged. To this day I love him for this. He proved that he was understanding, reasonable, tender, and a true Christian, without being overly pious. We often went on family outings, picnics, excursions on a lake. Together we played games. Quiet, guessing, loud, laughing, running, screaming, funny games! Mother was heaps of fun. Our house rang with much laughter. We went to concerts, to Chautauquas, to lectures, and to conferences. I learned to appreciate the common, the finer, and the finest things in life. In my early teens I was given three music lessons a week, two of voice and one of piano. Also some elocution lessons; "for the glory of God" Papa said they must be.

* * *

We had our first date on September 16, the year Norman and

I were both sixteen. For months we had been looking forward to the day when our parents would give us approval for more than walking to and from school together. We were extremely happy.

"Let's make sixteen our special number and day from this night on," Norman said.

"Let's do," I agreed.

For the next five years we celebrated on every sixteenth. Gifts mounted high. So did the love letters with sixteen scribbled on every page. When Norman worked at Kunderd's gladiolus farm, he brought me sixteen stems of beautiful glads every Saturday night.

After graduation my job was serving as cashier in Drake's Department Store, and it was a most fascinating one. From the overhanging balcony where I made change I could see hundreds of items to beautify any home. Since I got a liberal discount on any item, I decided to start our collection. Norman worked in a hardware store across the street. He too got a discount. What a break!

But Norman kept saying that he felt called to go to India someday as a missionary. I was utterly disappointed. I did not want to go to India, where it was hot and "insecty" and dusty, and where I might have to live in a mud hut. I wanted a home here, filled with nice, comfortable, and not cheap things. Whenever the subject came up, I'd say, "If I go to India, I will go just to be with you, because I love you."

"But if God calls me, and we're meant for each other, and I'm sure we are, I think God will—"

I knew full well the sum of his unfinished sentence. It raced through the stream of my consciousness with vivid, live, tormenting thoughts both day and night, even when we moved the last piece of furniture into our fully furnished seven-room house. The rugs, the drapes, and everything I worked hard for, looked so pretty—so fresh, so new. What a lovely home to be married in! April 16, 1924, while the hands of the clock were slowly moving upward for health, happiness, and a long prosperous life together. Was any couple ever happier?

Although we didn't agree one hundred per cent on the India

question, our love grew daily. After all, what couple does agree on every minute detail? "Can't we be missionaries right here at home?" I reasoned. "God calls many to support others. Why can't you be satisfied to support two or three? Anyhow I doubt if I'd live long in India."

"Then I'll work hard to support a couple," Norman said. We never missed morning worship, and we went faithfully to prayer meeting. Not to my inmost soul would I admit a hurting tinge of uneasiness. Yet at the most unexpected moment it screamed at me with sudden frightening closeness, "Unless you love me first and above all else"—"We gave you to God before"—"For a definite purpose. . . ."

* * *

Twenty-six months of married bliss. "Oh! No! No! Don't tell me! It can't be true! This is our day!"

But it was true.

The front page of the evening paper told the story in bold type above his picture. "Young businessman electrocuted this afternoon (June 16, 1926) while installing a radio."

Everything in the house turned to mud and ashes. Things I'd worked hard for meant absolutely nothing now. I hated the sight of it all. All, all I wanted taken from me? And on this, our day! O God!

Then a still small voice whispered within, "Not your day. All your days are my days. This is my doing."

I knew. It was the voice of Truth.

Hours later, dropping on my knees beside Norman's lifeless body I cried in anguish of soul, "Oh, if I had you back, I'd go to India. I'd gladly live in a mud hut. I'd sleep on a grass mat. If I had you back, I'd give up all this and go anywhere God called you. A thousand times I would."

God knew I meant it. But too late I stopped reasoning selfishly with my own conscience. Too late I was ready to set my highest affection on things of highest value. No one needed to tell me. Inside a great bonfire was burning. Furniture, drapes, silver, and crystal could never make me happy. But full dedication, self-consecration would.

My church membership, my reading and praying, teaching, giving, going, singing, all my doings, were not enough. I lacked the thing of most importance. Oh, for that early lighthearted freedom from fear!

For two years I lived under the torturous conviction that my life's purpose was ruined. All I could hear were those sixteen letters pounding like mad: "If I had you back now." I wrote pages giving expression to my pressed and bleeding heart, then tore them to shreds.

One evening, while running the hemstitching machine in the Singer shop, wondering if I would be spending the remainder of my life making frivolous organdy ruffles, the phone rang. A local minister invited me to go along to Hesston College, where he was to be an instructor in the six weeks' Bible term. Would I? I had never dreamed of such a thing. Could I? I called the store manager. He agreed to give me six weeks' leave. Long before the Bible term ended I had determined to prepare for definite Christian service. I handed God my last key. I'd go to the back sticks, the mountains, the jungles, India, Africa, or to an old people's home! If nothing more, I'd get down on my knees and scrub for God. Just to know I was forgiven for my selfish, obstinate attitude, and would still be accepted for some type of service, was all I wanted. I knew I'd go alone. Just God and I.

I wrote my boss that I would not be back.

Ten months later Nelson took me to a concert. He told me with tenderness how my testimony in Missionary Band interested and thrilled him (little did I imagine it!) and how he had purchased two tickets to the concert, and had prayed over them for two weeks with me in mind. Me? A poor widow? In the months following every star in the sky helped God tell me that I was forgiven, accepted, and that all I had buried was coming to life again. Only this was a richer, fuller, sweeter, more meaningful life. Oh, to be loved again! To be wanted! To have a God-fearing, consecrated friend who craved my kind of love. We believed alike. His convictions were my convictions. We knew that God had made and kept us for each other. June 10, 1929, we said our vows.

Nelson made a beautiful buffet out of orange crates. Our first drapes were crepe paper. We were happier than millionaires.

I knelt beside him when he was ordained to the ministry in 1934, and again as bishop in 1940. Both times I told God, "You have first right to him." I was happy and content to take second place. Twenty-two blessed years we served together in Hannibal, Missouri. Many times I prayed with childlike faith, expecting the answer. Marvelous were His answers beyond expectation. It would take volumes to relate them.

Not one thing have I of which to boast. I never deserved all these wonderful mercies. Why has He blessed me so? Why was I born in a happy Christian home? Why was I given a second chance? I'll never know. This one thing I do know, I'll be forever amazed and grateful. But unless I give God first place, He has no place at all. This is my greatest temptation.

Yes, it was in my home I first met God. It was there I felt, I saw, I learned, what He is like. The church was only another place to worship. I pray that our children will be able to say the same.

13
Saved and Led

WILLARD S. KRABILL

I was fortunate in being born and reared in a fine Christian home, where I received Christian training both by teaching and by example. From my earliest remembrance, the precepts and principles of Christ were taught to me. My conception of Jesus was always personal; I knew of Him as a Friend, one to whom I could always turn for help.

My conversion, therefore, was typical of that of most young people reared in such a Christian atmosphere. It was the climax of a prolonged, gradual process. I had always been rather quiet, reserved, and "well behaved"; but I was, of course, "born in sin," and was continually sinning. I was, therefore, a sinner in need of forgiveness, and gradually this realization bore down upon me. For quite a while previous to my conversion I had a great desire to do something about it and to make things right. For example, each year our church sponsored evangelistic meetings. Each year the visiting evangelist affected me more and more. The messages touched me more each year, but I did not accept Christ. Something held me back. Perhaps the custom of many in our congregation of joining church at twelve years of age had something to do with my hesitancy.

One year before my conversion the evangelist was a very con-

Willard S. and Grace Hershberger Krabill live in Goshen, Indiana, with their three children, a son and two daughters. He is currently president of the Mennonite Medical Association and a member of the Committee on Medicine and Religion of the American Medical Association.

servative man, and once during his meetings he denounced the wearing of trunks on the basketball floor. At this stage in the process leading to my conversion I was very sensitive, and his words worked on me until I decided not to wear trunks any more. I was on my elementary school basketball team, and although it made me embarrassingly conspicuous, I stood firm on my decision, and wore knickers while all the others wore trunks. This is just an example of my growing religious consciousness, as it moved from the peripheral to the center of my life.

In all this, my parents neither discouraged nor encouraged me. Although they did not feel as I did about the matter, they encouraged me to do as I felt best. I knew their sincere desire was that I should find Christ, and that they prayed to that end, but the decision was left to me.

I made my decision for Christ a year later, when I was twelve years old. As I was the first convert in that series of evangelistic meetings, I was not influenced by the decisions of any friends. It was my own decision, brought about by the Spirit of God. The prolonged, gradual process of conviction of sin, a growing sense of insecurity, inadequacy, defeat, and remorse, was climaxed, and I suddenly became free and extremely happy. I, too, became in tune with all that is good, beautiful, and worthy in the universe. I was redeemed; I was free from condemnation.

As is true in most conversion experiences, I did not fully understand the doctrine of salvation, or any other theological aspects of my conversion. I did not fully know what was meant by atonement and redemption, nor did I know fully in what way Jesus was my Saviour, but I did know that I had made the right decision, that I did the will of God, and that Jesus was "mine." The years since my conversion experience have been years of growing awareness of the constant leading of God in my life. This leading has come in myriads of ways through the months and years. I have learned through some painful experiences to be patient in awaiting the working out of God's will and the manifestation of this leading. Each time that I have become impatient, taking things in my own hands and pushing ahead on a given plan, I have had cause for regret. There have been mistakes, and I have transgressed against others many times in the ensuing years. For these offenses, however, I have the assurance of the forgiveness of Him who called me to be His at my conversion.

A major crisis occurred when I was twenty-three. A career in medicine had been my intention for some years, although I was not determined that this was the only avenue of service for me. This calling was seriously challenged the summer prior to my entrance to medical school by close friends who felt certain that I should abandon my place in the freshman class of Jefferson Medical College in order to become a minister in my home congregation. At the same time there was also much encouragement on the part of the Goshen College administration and faculty for me to prepare for a teaching assignment there. This difficult summer was taken up as a member of a Peace Team, sponsored by the Peace Problems Committee, touring Midwestern churches. And all the while we traveled, the decision had to be made as to my destination in September.

It was significant to me that I was chosen for medical school from among five thousand applicants. Our freshman class of 160 represented about three per cent of those who had applied. My interest in teaching was largely my interest in Goshen College, rather than in teaching as a profession. I realized that I could not count on teaching on one particular campus all my life, the vicissitudes of a professor's life on a denominational campus being what they are. Furthermore, family involvements and other personality factors in the local church scene seemed to indicate that the pastorate there was not the calling for me. Thus I was led to medical school and to a career of service in the medical profession.

I give this story in some detail because it is typical of the way God has led in my life. First is the quandary, the seemingly insoluble dilemma, the fork in the road ahead. Then there are the voices of trusted advisers and friends, each often urging a different course. Then comes the period of waiting, thinking, praying, weighing, and further waiting—even waiting while some opportunities pass one by, and doors close. But finally, one course seems most wise, most opportune, most needful, or most clear. No bells ring, no visions are experienced, but a way becomes clearer through experiences, circumstances, and growing internal conviction. This is how my life has been led by God for twenty-five years and I share this with others whose lives may have been or will be similarly led.

So it was that I entered medical school. By a similar process of leading I was able to make decisions as to summer employment during medical school vacations, was enabled to take an internship near my Ohio home, found an opportunity in private practice with two other experienced physicians (both Christians) which involved no financial investment, thus paving the way for easy acceptance of a hoped-for church service assignment. At this time God again used unusual circumstances to bring me to know the girl who became my wife and we "honeymooned" on our way to Southeast Asia on an MCC assignment (Mennonite Central Committee is the all-Mennonite relief agency). Meanwhile, the science faculty at Goshen College was strengthened by God-directed additional persons who are convinced and expert teachers. And a year after my entrance to medical school one of my best friends accepted the call to the pastorate of my home congregation, a young man far better suited than I to meet the spiritual needs of that group.

Ever since Goshen College days, I had been interested in foreign service under church auspices. My participation in the 1948 European Student Tour work camp only intensified this interest. Then, annually, during my medical school days in Philadelphia, J. D. Graber kept this interest growing by keeping us aware of the church's service opportunities and interest in each of us.

In the spring of 1955 I agreed to go to Puerto Rico to fill a sudden need for a physician there. I disposed of my practice and made arrangements to go, but then the urgent need in Puerto Rico disappeared by the reversal of the government's attitude regarding the physician already there. There I was, all packed and ready to go, my medical practice disposed of, my wedding in the offing. A telephone call a day later from Orie O. Miller in Chicago told of the urgent need in Vietnam for medical services, and of MCC's desire for me to open a medical program there. God had led again into an unexpected venture, one into which we felt directly called.

Our three years' service in Vietnam was difficult, and demanded more patience than I could ever have possessed of myself.

The months of waiting for approval by this or that official, or this or that board, lengthened into years, and we never did get to see the final completion of the hospital we had set out to build. It was dedicated after our return home. But because we waited, because God gave us His peace, and His patience, a confidence was established between the Christian and Missionary Alliance and the Mennonites which has enabled our continued co-operation in Vietnam, and in 1960 led Christian and Missionary Alliance officials in the Congo to request MCC help there, "similar to that given in Vietnam."

For one as interested as I am in the work of foreign missions and relief, and as aware as I am of the critical need for physicians in many parts of the world, my private practice in a comfortable Midwestern town seems incongruous. Yet at a crucial point in our deciding what to do upon our return to the United States in 1958, the call came to come to Goshen. The timing of this was clearly a divine intervention in our carefully laid plans. Then came the additional call to leadership in the Mennonite Medical Association at a turning point in the life of this organization, plus the opportunity at Goshen to work with those making their own life decisions, and with those who help their students make their life decisions.

Meanwhile God has prospered my practice so that other physicians are needed to carry it on, and these physicians are proving to be available in a marvelous, God-directed way. This, in turn, will enable me and my colleagues to be of further service to the church it its relief and mission programs, as God may lead.

Just as God has led in my service for Him, He has also led in my life union with Him, and my faith in Him. His care and leading have built within the life of this one of His followers a confidence which enables me to look ahead without fear. This faith has been tested, but God through Christ has been faithful, so that I have confidence in Him for all the days ahead. His faithfulness in all of my past life makes my future life with Christ one of eager anticipation, knowing something of how He can bless one small life like mine in such wonderful ways. Any accomplishments are truly His. It has only been His intervention in my life that has kept it from being a life of unhappiness, frustration, and bitterness.

14
Called to Serve the Church

JOHN E. LAPP

Unlike the majority of Mennonite boys of my generation, it was my privilege to grow to manhood in a town instead of on a farm. The town of Lansdale had a population of 2,500 when I was a growing boy; today that population is multiplied by five. The center of activity in those days was a busy railroad station in the center of town, with the large livery stable one block west, where all the horses coming into town were stabled, and where the buggies were stored. The three hotels [saloons] were always busy in the preprohibition days. My home was along the main street, only three blocks from the center of the town, and my parents were deeply conscious of the evil influences so prevalent in that day, and the dangers amidst which their children were growing up.

There was no Mennonite church in the town in those days. Our church, the Plains Mennonite Church, was located west of the town, about a mile from our home. Every Sunday Father would hitch up the horse and drive to the church services, taking Mother and all the children, plus other residents of the town. Worship services were held every other Sunday, but Sunday school was conducted every Sunday, with the exception of several months during the winter.

When I was four years old, Father suffered a severe case of diphtheria. He never fully recovered from this illness; after this he

---

John E. Lapp is moderator of the Franconia Mennonite Conference, a leader in his denomination, and a member of many church committees.

conducted a retail produce route in town, and on Saturdays and in summertime I had the happy privilege of going with him on his route. When I was but eight years old, Father died very suddenly one evening, a half hour after he had retired for the night. His death was the most difficult adjustment of my whole life, for I could not believe that Father was dead. I felt that it was but a dream, and that soon he would return. Father did not return. Yet I have carried with me through life the most pleasant memories of a loving father who cared for me.

Father spent the evenings at home with his family. I can still hear him singing, "My Faith Looks Up to Thee" and "Rock of Ages," and can still see lying on the living room table the Bible which he regularly read. And I can still feel some of the corrections which he gave to me—the whipping that he gave me when I had taken some of his money and spent it for myself. This he administered in the house when my brother and sister were not at home. I have felt Father's love, Father's concern, and Father's prayers as they followed me all through my life experiences.

My mother, Kate Clemmer Lapp, was a very resourceful woman. In the early part of the century it was quite common when a parent died for children to be placed in foster homes that they might work and make their own way through life. I shall always be grateful to my mother, who worked hard, lived frugally, and kept her children with her until they were grown to manhood and womanhood. There were many lessons in life—moral training, spiritual enlightenment, honesty as a principle of life, good saving and spending habits, the meaning of the separated life, and the total meaning of brotherhood in the church—which are much better learned from one's mother than from any other influences or schools. Through Mother's influence I was kept from many evils of life as a growing boy. She did not permit her children to attend the movies, even though our home was only two blocks from the theater, and Mother was a close friend of the wife of the operator, visiting her frequently and entertaining her quite often. Mother assumed the full responsibility for guiding her children after Father's death. The product of her training may speak to the degree of her success.

As children we had few playthings from the store. We made our own games, and played with neighbor children in the back alley. I vividly remember an experience which occurred when I was in the first grade. Gas mains were being put underground in the street in the next block above our home. The open trench gathered much water from excessive rains, and neighbor boys were sailing boats on the water. When they could not reach the boat, I said that I could, but I stretched too far, falling into the water headfirst. Returning to my own back yard I tried to dump the water out of my shoes, and was in the midst of drying my clothes when Mother, who never missed anything, saw me. She called me into the house, had me undress in the kitchen, took down the paddle from above the kitchen range where it was always kept, and warmed me up. This incident I have never forgotten, but unfortunately I may not have learned all of the lessons which I should have learned, because I have all too often "stuck my neck out" since that day.

After Father's death I spent many happy hours with my eighty-year-old grandfather. I used to curry his horses and mow his lawn. I remember a severe scolding he gave me one day because, having gone to play with some other boys, I did not mow the lawn when he wanted me to. I used to sit by the hour listening to Grandfather tell me stories of the development of Lansdale, and of his own experiences during the Civil War. He said that on several occasions he paid $300 as a commutation fee to relieve him of military service. As a ten-year-old boy I talked very much with Grandfather about World War I, which was then raging in Europe. Grandfather died at about the time the United States entered World War I; he did not live through those days of warm expressions of patriotism in these United States.

When I was fourteen years old, Mother bought a five-year-old Model T Ford touring car. This she bought so that, instead of walking, our family might be able to ride to church again, which we had not been doing for several years after the family carriage and horse were disposed of. We used this Model T to drive to church and to do some visiting of relatives. This also made it possible for us to attend the special meetings which were just beginning in Eastern Pennsylvania with the establishment of a district mission board and the opening of the first mission at Norristown. We frequently attended evangelistic meetings at Norristown, and attended a few special meetings in some of the other churches some distance from our home. Hearing the evangelistic appeals brought a fourteen-year-old boy to the place where he saw himself as a sinner before God, but he was unwilling to break with sin. He heard the claims that Christ presented to him in sermon and song, but was not willing to commit his life to Christ. Such evangelists as John W. Hess and John F. Bressler personally invited this boy to Christ during meetings at the Norristown Mission. But he said no to them and to the Holy Spirit.

This rejection of the Saviour, which continued for about two years, meant that Satan was getting a stronger hold. Among other sins his speech became profane. He did not speak the truth to his mother and his teachers. He became a sneak at smoking and pitching pennies. He was living a double life. Those who saw him on Sunday thought he was a good boy, but those who knew him on other days knew that he was a bad boy, and the longer he resisted the wooing of the Spirit of God, the deeper he became involved in sin and in all of its entanglements.

From the background of these, my own experiences, I have felt a deeper understanding of human nature. I am not as inclined as many to justify my boys with the excuse, "They are such good boys!" Watching my sons growing to manhood, I have repeatedly seen my own life to some extent lived over in them. These experiences have also given me a better understanding of the needs of youth as I continue to minister among them.

My conversion was not nearly as dramatic as the experience of the man who has been a drunkard in the gutter, a gambler in the den, or a vice-loving one living in the haunts of sin. I did, however, need to experience the forgiveness of sins, cleansing by the blood of Jesus Christ, and the grace of God for my own salvation. This has always been real to me, even though Satan has attempted to upset my faith on many occasions by the worst forms of doubt.

J. C. Clemens, who has been my elder brother in the ministry for thirty years, the pastor of the congregation where I was growing to manhood, and a close family friend, spoke to me on several occasions inviting me to come to the Lord. This was to be expected of him, for he was actively engaged in evangelistic work, even before the 1920's. My answer used to be, "I want to, but I don't want to be the only one of my age group." On a Wednesday morning before I left home for high school, Brother Clemens stopped in at our home and told me that his sixteen-year-old son had responded to the Gospel invitation, and he invited me to respond also. I could resist no longer and said, "I will come and follow my Lord." On the following Saturday, June 9, 1921, baptism was administered during preparatory services (the day before the communion service) in the Plains Church, and I was in the number without having been instructed in the usual instruction class. Jonas Mininger, the bishop resident in the Plains Mennonite Church, Lansdale, who always preached in German, baptized me upon the confession of my faith in Jesus Christ. Brother Mininger was at that time the senior bishop and the moderator of the Franconia Conference. (Little did I realize as a fifteen-year-old boy that in twelve years I would become his successor in the ministry, in sixteen years his successor as bishop, and in thirty-four years the moderator of the Franconia Conference.) When the congregation sang, "O Happy Day," I could join in the singing of this hymn wholeheartedly because of the experience of joy that I had in my own soul.

I participated in my first foot-washing service that day, and in the communion services on the day following, just three months before I reached the age of sixteen. My life was now different in this respect: I had victory over some temptations that I did not have victory over before, such as smoking and profanity. My next school year began to mean something to me, and the last two years of my high-school experience were worth while. My only regret is that I didn't give my heart to God in full surrender at the beginning of my high-school days, for then my first two years of high school could have been different, and could have been a profitable experience for me instead of being simply an unpleasant memory. After my conversion I found it necessary to make restitution for many wrongs to schoolteachers, businessmen, and others. But this brought peace to my soul.

After graduating from high school in June, 1923, I found employment in a small mill in Lansdale, doing both office work and some supervisory work in the mill. As I did not like the confinement there, I found other employment and operated a bread route for three and one-half years. Then followed three years working in a tile plant in Lansdale. There was a sense of restlessness in my life, because I was aware that I had not yet found my niche. God was calling. God was speaking to me. I left the tile plant and began to operate a small grocery store in Lansdale in 1930.

After a courtship of almost three years I took in marriage the hand of Edith R. Nyce on September 15, 1926. Before our wedding day I told her of how the Lord was leading my life, and that sometime He would be calling me into some place of Christian service, such as the ministry. Together we dedicated our lives to the Lord, saying to Him, "We will go where you want us to go, we will do what you want us to do, we will be what you want us to be, we will say what you want us to say." We did not know what this dedication might lead us into. With our naive promise in this act of dedication to God, we made a commitment as Abraham did when he left his own country and went into a land which he did not know.

Eleven times my good wife has gone into the mysterious realms of motherhood and has brought back with her a darling baby. On two occasions these beautiful well-formed little sons did not draw a breath. We have today five sons and four daughters scattered across our country and as far south as Honduras in Christian service and witness. Mother has been the one who nurtured her children, while Father was gone much of the time through their growing years from infancy to manhood. She must be given much of the credit for their interest in the work of the Lord, and their service in His kingdom.

On June 22, 1933, the Plains Mennonite Church called for a minister. The second youngest of six brethren to share the lot on that occasion, I took the only book that remained after the five others had chosen their books. In my book the bishop, Jonas

Mininger, found the paper which indicated God's choice for this service. I have never doubted God's call in my life of ministerial service. No matter what discouragements came my way, or how much opposition I was called upon to face, or how difficult the financial struggles which our family experienced, God's call was always real to me. This was assuredly God's call for my life in service to Him.

The evident leading of the Lord continued. Less than four years later, on June 1, 1937, I was again separated unto new responsibilities, being chosen a bishop in the Middle District of the Franconia Conference. The ordination occurred in the Franconia meetinghouse, where I was again one of six ministers (this time the youngest) who shared the lot, and again had no choice of a book, simply taking the one that remained. This call also has never been questioned in the past quarter century of my ministry.

Very early in my ministry I became involved in missions and evangelism, and I participated in the missionary outreach of the Franconia Conference, assisting in a number of the mission points. In addition to serving in my home conference I have also been engaged in Bible conference and evangelistic work in a dozen other states. Returning home by train after what seemed to be a successful series of evangelistic meetings some years ago, I encountered one of the most severe conflicts of my life. After this series of meetings, coming face to face with Satan in a real way was a trial for me. When one leaves a strenuous meeting, tired, exhausted, and homesick for his family, and then faces Satan's supreme efforts to overthrow his faith, it is surely one of the fiery trials of which Peter writes.

Through a serious church trial in the Franconia Conference in recent years, God has been teaching me the need for unity in the body of Christ. My life has been dedicated to the cause of maintaining the unity of the Spirit in the bond of peace. When one sees the breaking of hearts, homes, lives, and congregations, as individuals break fellowship with the church, it is disturbing to one's peace of mind. As I look back to the years of my ministry, I sometimes wonder whether I have been as much interested in souls, that is, persons, as I have been in a cause. It is souls for whom Christ died, it is souls who compose the body of Christ, and it is souls who will spend eternity as the glorified saints of God in the presence of the glorified Lamb of God. As one looks back through the history of the church, and sees the many historical accidents of division, he senses a tragedy. My life is dedicated to the cause of unity in the brotherhood.

Through the years of my ministry I have been known as a "progressive conservative." It is to be expected that one in this category will see changes effected. During the years, leadership has been given to the enlargement of the mission program, the encouragement of evangelistic meetings in every congregation, the establishment of such young people's activities as young people's institute and MYF, and of Christian day schools, both elementary and secondary. There has also been an increasing number of study conferences in various areas of church practice, provision for mass evangelism, and a greater development of organizations and committees throughout the conference.

I still hear the voice of God speaking to me. On several occasions I experienced a complete stop in my life, such as being hospitalized for what was diagnosed as an aneurysm in the brain. On all of these occasions of a "stop," and especially this one, I went through personal heart-searching and a review of my own life and relations to God, as well as the situation of my family if this should be the time of my departure. Such a sweet peace and blessed assurance swept over my soul that I have always felt that these experiences were good for me.

Five brethren have made an outstanding contribution to my life. These are John L. Stauffer, former president, and Chester K. Lehman, former dean of Eastern Mennonite College, who so kindly welcomed me into their circle, and Harold S. Bender, Orie O. Miller, and Amos S. Horst, with whom I served as a member of the Peace Problems Committee for more than twenty years. These, together with many other brethren, have had a tremendous influence upon me, and helped to prepare me for broader fields of service. I have accepted the call to be a committeeman in the church, and a conference leader, as a serious charge. This has challenged me to give of my best to His service.

15

From National Socialism to Christian Faith

FRED LINHART

I was born in Dresden, capital city of Saxony, on November 30, 1913. My parents were separated when I was five years old. My father then moved to Cologne and remarried. I cannot remember ever hearing a prayer offered in our home. My stepmother was a Catholic, and I was sent to a Catholic school of higher education in Czechoslovakia. At first I liked this school very much, and was willing to study for the Catholic priesthood. The beauty of the worship ceremony, the solemn behavior, and the reverence in the church made a deep impression upon me. In the course of time, however, I became disturbed and disappointed by the conduct of my superiors. Ultimately this destroyed my tender growing faith. I made the decision to discontinue my studies, and began to serve as an apprentice with a small glass company.

In my search for a new ideal, I found it in the person of the German party leader, Adolf Hitler. He spoke of freedom for the German nation, the end of unemployment, and of a happy future for all the people. This vision warmed my heart, and on March 21, 1933, I went to Potsdam in order to see the *Führer*. When I saw him come out of the old church where the *Reichstag* met, my heart was so filled with enthusiam that I was convinced of the rightness

---

Fred Linhart lives with his family near Toledo, Ohio. He is deeply grateful that God brought him to a land of liberty, and much more, to a living faith in Christ and a happy church fellowship.

and honesty of the man and of his program. Consequently, when the war broke out, I gladly volunteered to serve in the army to help destroy the greatest enemy of Hitler, the Soviet Union. It is not my intention here to describe the events of World War II, which were truly horrible. When I think of those years, I can still hear the cries of helpless victims, and remember the mass murder by both sides, and the injustice to, and the terror of, innocent people.

However, the worst came only with the end of the war. The chastisement of the Lord fell upon the country. Many people committed suicide. I myself was in a state of deep distress. Everything in which I had believed existed no more. I was extremely confused, and had no sense of a foundation under my feet. What is really right? What is the purpose of this life? If there is a God, how could it be possible that we Germans should lose, and the communists win the war? For me it was questions, questions, questions—all without an answer.

God finally led me to the home of an elderly Christian couple in the city of Kassel, a couple whose only son did not return from a flight over Russian territory. This home provoked new questions in my mind. Why, I asked myself, did people with such a fine Christian home, with a son so much beloved by his parents, have to lose their boy? And why should I, who had nothing to lose, survive? Furthermore, how could these people be so calm, and whence did they get their faith?

I asked them many questions which they patiently tried to answer for me. They told me how our nation had rejected the holy God, and instead had worshiped a man. They also spoke to me of the love of God for all men, and of our human sinfulness.

In the room where I lived, that of their son, a verse hung over the door which read in German: "God is our refuge and strength, a very present help in trouble" (Psalm 46:1). Oh, I thought, if I could only believe that! Surely a refuge is what I needed. Help in all my troubles was what I was looking for. But where was God, and how could I find Him?

This dear couple told me that I would find all my answers in the Bible. They encouraged me to read it. I did not accompany them to church, but one Sunday morning when they were at church,

I took the Bible and looked for contradictory statements to convince myself that the Bible was not true! Upon opening the Scriptures, my eyes fell upon the statement in bold print: "Jesus saith unto him, I am the way, the truth, and the life: no man cometh unto the Father, but by me" (John 14:6).

These words shocked me! Here was someone saying, "I am the way." If this were true, then Hitler was not the way. Here indeed was a Person who claimed to be the truth and the life, but the question still haunted me, What is the purpose of life? Why did so many good people have to die?

I was so confused that I left the home of my Christian friends, and decided to go to the East Zone of Germany. Perhaps I would be able to find out what had happened to their son. Crossing the border secretly had never been a big problem for me. Therefore, I was completely taken aback and disconcerted when a Russian soldier suddenly stood before me with his gun aimed at me. After he asked me why I was in East Germany, he became suspicious and led me to his superior. For days the commissar tried to get a confession from me. He accused me of being a spy sent by the English army. He could not read English, and so when I showed him my release paper as a prisoner of war, he did not believe me. My admission to him that I had been a former Nazi was proof, so far as he was concerned, that I was a war criminal. During those days as a prisoner of the Russians, I often thought of the words which I had read in the Bible, "I am the way, the truth, and the life."

Finally the day came when I was led to a brick wall in the yard. The commissar told me that I had five minutes in which to confess my guilt or be shot. Facing the wall, I awaited the final sound of his gun. My thoughts went to God. Somehow I did not ask Him to spare my life, but only to reveal Himself to me, and to be merciful to me. I prayed: "O God, let me find the way and the truth."

Suddenly I heard the sound of an approaching car and a man calling out in Russian. I turned my head and saw a high-ranking officer standing upright in his car and talking to my guard. After examining my prisoner of war release paper, he shouted something, and returned the document to the guard. As the guard came toward me, he said, "Here is your paper. Get out of here and never come back."

I could hardly believe it. God surely must have heard my prayer! I was now free to go. My heart was full of gratitude to Him. He truly was a refuge in time of trouble! That very night I returned to the West Zone. I then found a job as a glazier in a small town. The first Sunday, when the bells rang for morning worship, I went to church to give thanks to God, and to hear more about Him. The old church was full of people. I found a seat in the back. The minister spoke clearly, and I felt that he spoke only to me. He mentioned the sin of our nation, how we had worshiped a man, and the great multitude of innocent people who had to die because of their refusal to co-operate with the wicked regime of the country. He humbled himself as he confessed his neglect in not preaching the truth more effectively. He asked God's forgiveness for his sins, and for the sins of the German people.

I was deeply moved. Never before in my life had I heard such a sermon. I looked around and saw tears on many faces. In my heart I was also silently weeping. Everything the man had said was very true. After that day, I did not miss a single service.

One Sunday, after the church service, I asked the minister how I could become a Christian. He invited me to his study in his home. I visited him a number of times. One evening as we read from the Bible, the pastor came upon the words: "If we walk in the light, as he is in the light, we have fellowship one with another, and the blood of Jesus Christ his Son cleanseth us from all sin" (I John 1:7).

I could hardly comprehend these words and asked him to read that sentence again. Sure enough, it really said *all sin*. I was not mistaken. How could I believe that? I told the pastor that I was really a great sinner, and wished that that promise might also include me. He replied, "When it says all sin, it means just that, and nothing else. Your sins, my sins, and the sins of the whole world."

We got down on our knees together and I prayed that God might give me faith personally to accept His Word. I told God that I was a poor man, and needed much forgiveness. He gave me in that moment the assurance of His forgiving grace. How my heart was filled with praise and thanksgiving! The pastor and his family rejoiced with me.

When I left that home, I was a new creature in Christ Jesus, my Lord and Saviour. My soul was singing. I read much in the Scriptures, and especially enjoyed the Psalms. And what a wonderful spirit is to be found in the Sermon on the Mount! Here is truth. I had been longing for it for a long time. And how precious were the letters of Paul! What a harmony of spirit runs through the whole Bible! Truly, this is God's Word to all mankind.

In 1954 my family and I migrated to Canada. In Winnipeg we had our first contact with Mennonites. In 1956 I received an offer of employment in a large glass company in Toledo, Ohio. I felt that it was the leading of the Lord to accept this offer. And once again, it was a Mennonite minister who was the first Christian to visit our home. The spirit of love brought us closer together, and in 1958 my wife and I united with the Mennonite brotherhood.

Words cannot express the wonder of finding the Lord. It is my wish that all who have experienced the abundant grace of our Saviour, the Lord Jesus Christ, might be living witnesses for Him, so that seeking souls might see Him in their lives.

(Compare the fuller account in the book by Christmas Carol Kauffman, *For One Moment,* Herald Press, 1960.)

16
Called to International Witness

NELSON LITWILLER

I was born on February 16, 1898, on a farm near St. Agatha, Ontario, about seven miles west of Kitchener, the county seat. My great-grandfather, Peter Litwiller, was born in Alsace, and as a nonresistant Christian came to Canada to avoid military service. This Peter Litwiller, who was born on January 8, 1809, and who died July 7, 1878, was not only a frontiersman, a land-clearing pioneer, but also became a bishop in the Amish Mennonite Church, and a respected leader in the community. When the funeral procession, en route to the cemetery, passed in front of the Roman Catholic Church, the parish priest had the church doors opened and the bells tolled in his honor.

Peter's son, Christian, my grandfather, who was born in 1852 and died in 1924, was a minister in the same Amish congregation for many years. My father, Jacob Litwiller, who was born in 1874 and died in 1928, was not a minister but was vitally interested in the activities of the church. Since my grandfather was a minister, and my father was the oldest son in his family, I remember that Grandpa would come across the fields to our house and discuss church work and problems. In this way, early in life, I was introduced to the work and problems of the church. So from my earliest childhood I was almost involuntarily involved in the ecclesiastical, theological, and church administration problems of the time.

Nelson Litwiller serves as Field Secretary for South America of the Mennonite Board of Missions and Charities, Elkhart, Indiana, and as president of the Mennonite Seminary in Montevideo, Uruguay.

Our church would today be considered very conservative in practice. I remember when I was five years old my father came home on a below-zero evening from hauling logs to town. He wore a peaked cap that had flaps for the ears. He had discarded his broad-brimmed hat because he had frozen his ears several times. The transition from a hat to a cap became the subject of serious discussion, and I lost sleep fearing that my father would be excommunicated from the church! The first coat I wore to public school had hooks and eyes, instead of buttons, and so when buttons did creep into the church, there were also times of serious discussion. In fact, church life was a perennial struggle between the more liberal and the more conservative or "status quo" elements who clashed over such innovations as top buggies, telephones, "shingled" hair for men, neckties, Sunday schools, young people's Bible meetings, English preaching, automobiles, and capes and bonnets for women. The situation seemed quite serious, and the opposing elements were so irreconcilable that for a period of time in the years 1914 and 1915 outside bishop help was called in, and our home bishop, Daniel Steinman, was silenced. Bishops D. J. Johns of Indiana and E. L. Frey of Ohio made periodic visits, and in due time the leadership was returned to Bishop Steinman. It was during E. L. Frey's visits and special ministry that a large class of converts, of which my wife and I were members, was baptized.

Another factor from my early childhood experience should be mentioned because of its influence upon my life. My father was an avid reader, and was much interested in community and world affairs. Even though voting was at that time frowned upon, and but few members of our church, as far as I know, participated in elections, my father took a keen interest in the political issues of the day. It was the custom at that time that the citizens of the county who were running for Parliament would come to the village and in the evening would hold political meetings in the hall above the blacksmith shop. Even though I was rather young, my father took me with him. The public debate made a tremendous impression on my life, intrigued me, and aroused my interest in a Parliamentary career, and this in turn led to my decision to enter high school.

Since higher education was a thing unheard of in our congregation, my decision to go to high school was the occasion for much comment in the church. The mitigating factor was that the Amish ministers who had come to visit in Canada, men such as D. D. Miller of Indiana, had been schoolteachers. My father's youngest brother, only three years my senior, and a close pal, and I were the only ones from that congregation who went to high school and on to normal school. And for many years I was the only one from that church who continued in college and seminary.

The first spiritual stirrings in my heart and soul had come to me as my parents would take me with them to revival meetings which were held at the Shantz Mennonite Church, located only two miles west of our farm. This was in the decade of the three-day Bible conferences which were followed by revival meetings in the evenings. These meetings influenced my parents. I remember distinctly that when I was eight years of age, and an invitation was given, I felt God's call to me even as He had called Samuel. But for a child of eight to stand, and make a profession of faith and be baptized, was unheard of in our circles, and because I was too timid to confide in anyone, the effect of the Spirit's call was, for me, quenched. Then in the course of my high-school career, I became involved with the wrong crowd, and participated in the activities of my group, smoking, social drinking, attendance at movies, and parties. The climax came when many of my high-school pals enlisted and served as soldiers in World War I. Since I was too young to enlist, I secretly joined a high-school training corps in preparation for military service. On training days I donned the uniform and marched up and down the streets of our city, which was then called Berlin [now Kitchener]. Ultimately, someone saw me in practice, and in due time this information was passed on to my parents. I knew all the while that my life was not right, and that I was drifting into sin. Cigarette smoking, for example, had become quite a habit for me, which I found myself unable to break, much as I tried to.

In the winter of 1916 God in His mercy and providence sent one of His servants to the community in the person of E. J. Berkey. This brother held evangelistic meetings, first in the Shantz Church, then at Blenheim, at Kitchener, and possibly in other congregations. Partly out of curiosity, and partly because I liked to listen to public speakers, I started to attend these meetings. It was early in one of these campaigns that God in His mercy and abundant grace worked effectively in my heart, and a sense of deep conviction for sin came over me. This process of conviction was persistent, unrelenting, and as it deepened, I tried to resist it. The odds seemed to be against me. To break with the training corps would be misunderstood. I would be called yellow, and I did not want to be a coward. To break with the pattern of living, and old friends, would be equally misunderstood. Since I was already a baptized member of the church, and took communion regularly, to make a confession of faith by the raising of the hand would certainly have been misunderstood and criticized by members of the Amish Church to which I belonged. And so it took weeks and weeks of intense struggle, of weighing the pros and cons, until finally on the last evening of the Kitchener series of meetings, in March, 1916, I made a public manifestation of my desire to follow Christ unreservedly. Dedicated Christians, ministers and lay brethren, prayed with me, encouraged me, and helped me, until I had the full assurance of sins forgiven and fellowship with Christ. This was a joyous and unforgettable experience in my life.

I resumed my high-school studies, the many feared obstacles were overcome, and I was really happy in my Christian life. My aim at that time was to become a schoolteacher, and I aspired in time to become a high-school teacher, and later perhaps inspector of schools, and even to enter public service or become a member of Parliament! (I was not aware then, even as I am not entirely convinced now, that a dedicated Christian cannot or should not be a faithful public servant.) So the blueprints for my life were clear, and within the framework of my Christian life.

In the fall of 1916, I. W. Royer came to the church known as the Baden Mission, Baden, Ontario, for a series of Bible studies and missionary messages. Mission work was relatively new in the church at that time. A few missionaries from India had indeed come through the community. Interest in foreign missions was growing in the church and there was a great need for workers. It had never occurred to me to become a minister, much less a foreign missionary. On the last night of his meetings Brother Royer asked for a public manifestation of volunteers. Two girls raised their hands, and Brother Royer, who was rather disappointed, in his unique way exclaimed, "How can you young men remain seated and let the girls be the volunteers!" At this point, the Holy Spirit clearly spoke to me, calling me to dedicate my life to the cause of Christ in some foreign field. Again I passed through an intense struggle, for I misunderstood, assuming that this dedication was tantamount to sailing the next month. Furthermore, my own plans for life could not then be realized. But again, kind friends and understanding brethren, who sensed and saw my predicament, gave me the necessary guidance and encouragement.

And so I finished my high-school studies, took one year of work at Stratford Normal School, and taught public school for one year at Petersburg, Ontario.

In April, 1919, a few months before public school closed, I was united in marriage with Ada Ramseyer, the loyal and self-sacrificing companion of my life. In September of 1919 we left Canada and entered Bethany Biblical Seminary in Chicago to prepare for foreign mission work. In the year 1920 we were in charge of the Twenty-sixth Street Mennonite Church. In order to meet the graduation requirements for the B.D. degree, and to become better acquainted with our own church, after finishing my seminary work in June, 1924, I entered Goshen College for a year of residence work. This was the year that the college had reopened under the presidency of S. C. Yoder. So in June of 1925 I graduated from Goshen with a B.A. degree, and a B.D. was granted me *in absentia* from Bethany. The year at Goshen was a spiritually enriching experience, which at the time gave me the needed orientation toward the church and her institutions. In 1925, at the Mission Board meeting at Harrisonburg, Virginia, we were appointed foreign missionaries. In June I was ordained to the ministry by Bishop D. A. Yoder of Elkhart, Indiana.

We sailed for South America from New York on September 5, 1925, and arrived in Buenos Aires on September 24. After living in Tres Lomas for a few months, we were transferred to

Pehuajo, where I became principal of the Bible School. During the years 1927 and 1928 we were in charge of the congregation in Trenque Lauquen, from whence I made weekly trips to teach in Pehuajo. In the year 1928 we were transferred to Pehuajo, where I had charge of the congregation and was director of the Bible School.

We had our first furlough in 1933. It was spent in extensive deputation work in Canada and the States, during which time I became better acquainted with our church at home. I also taught one semester in Goshen College at this time.

Our second term of service was a ten-year stint from 1934 to 1945, which time was spent as pastor of the Bragado Church, and principal of our Bible School. I also became secretary of the mission, and held power of attorney for the same.

On returning to the field in 1947, after a lengthy furlough during which I took a year of graduate study at Princeton Theological Seminary, we located in Bragado. It was from here that I made periodic visits to Uruguay, and by request of Mennonite Central Committee, contacted government ministries, and was able to obtain permits for the Danzig Mennonites to enter Uruguay en masse. This same year, 1947, I was ordained to the office of bishop. In 1949 we were asked to move to Buenos Aires to shepherd the scattered members who had moved to the capital in the exodus from our interior congregations. In the same year we organized the congregation, and bought the present property at Mercedes 149, Buenos Aires.

Our third furlough, 1952-53, was also dedicated to deputation work among the churches. (I was also a participant in the Mennonite World Conference held in Basel, Switzerland, in 1952.) While at home, I was appointed Field Secretary for lower Latin America for the Mennonite Board of Missions and Charities. I was also asked to organize a Seminary for the training of young people from our Mennonite constituency in Latin America. These two assignments of Field Secretary and President of the Seminary took me on periodic visits to Brazil, Paraguay, and Argentina. The Seminary was established at Montevideo, which became my home.

The Lord has truly been good to me. I rejoice in His service, and I count it a privilege to be considered worthy to be His servant.

17
My Conversion Experience

J. B. MARTIN

I was converted at the age of eighteen years. My parents belonged to a church that did not have Sunday schools, which meant that as a youth I received from the church very little Biblical teaching that was meaningful. My mother and father went to church regularly, and I have no reason to believe that they did not love the Lord, or were not in fellowship with Him. My life companion had had a similar background. Since the church did not contribute very much in teaching and nurturing, the age group to which I belonged drifted into sin.

Let me now relate definite factors that led me to accept Jesus Christ, "who hath delivered us from the power of darkness, and hath translated us into the kingdom of his dear Son: in whom we have redemption through his blood, even the forgiveness of sins" (Colossians 1:13, 14). My parents were grieved because I, with my friends, lived under the power of darkness. In fact, people were afraid of us because of the ungodly things we did and which we threatened to do. My parents were always kind to me, and in love talked to me of a better way of life than wayward prodigal living.

It was at this time that one of my chums invited me to Sunday school at the Old Conestoga Church, which is now the Mennonite Church in St. Jacobs. I expressed to my parents a desire to attend

---

J. B. Martin is a Christian minister in Waterloo, Ontario, and a leader in the Ontario Conference, the Mennonite General Conference, and the Mennonite World Conference.

Sunday school. They did not oppose my wish, but to my surprise, actually were glad and encouraged me to go. They had hoped somehow that I would break with the gang, which I did. This was not an easy thing to do, because now I became the target of ridicule and threatened persecution by my so-called friends. I began to attend Sunday school and church regularly. Soon my companions saw that I was sincere, and they let me alone. My good friend who invited me to Sunday school had an accident and died suddenly. God used this death to make me think. My friend was a Christian, and ready to die, but I had not yet accepted Christ. I read the Bible and studied the Sunday-school lessons, and read other Christian literature and books. The members of the church showed real Christian love toward me. All this background, which I have related as among the factors which led to my conversion, was of the Holy Spirit (John 16:7-11), reproving me of sin, of righteousness, and of judgment.

This was also the time in the history of the churches in Ontario when people looked forward to annual Bible conferences and revival meetings. The crowds and interest at these meetings impressed me, as a churchgoer. I witnessed a joy which I had not experienced. Daniel Kauffman held a series of meetings in the Waterloo Church. I attended a number of the evening meetings, and after the church service, Evangelist Kauffman would shake hands with the people at the back of the church building. When he shook my hand, he held it and asked, "Are you a Christian?" I replied, "No." He asked, "Would you like to become a Christian?" This was the first time in my life that an evangelist invited me to become a Christian, but I did not respond to the invitation.

In 1916 the well-known evangelist E. J. Berkey from Missouri held a series of meetings at the St. Jacobs Church. I attended every night and listened to the singing, praying, testimonies, and preaching. My mother kindly reminded me that this was the time to give my life to the Lord. She did not say very much, but again, as I review my past experience, I see that the Holy Spirit used people to witness to me about Christ and His salvation. I sat through that series of meetings, and listened to the messages of salvation, but I did not yield to the invitation to become a Christian until the evening before the meetings closed. I cannot recall a text, or any particular sermon, but I know many Christians were praying for me as the evangelist preached, and during the singing of the invitation hymn. The hymn I do remember:

"Softly and tenderly Jesus is calling,
Calling for you and for me;
See, on the portals He's watching and waiting,
Watching for you and for me.
Come home, come home,
Ye who are weary, come home!
Earnestly, tenderly, Jesus is calling,
Calling, O sinner, come home!"

Never will I forget how the devil held on to me, and what a freedom from sin I experienced as I stood to my feet and accepted and confessed Jesus Christ as Saviour. I never had any doubts from that hour until today that God forgave my sins, and made me a new creature in Christ as described in II Corinthians 5:14-21.

After my conversion the natural thing to do was to serve my Lord. I went through instruction class, listening to the exposition of the Eighteen Articles of Faith, commonly known as the Mennonite Confession of Faith (Dordrecht, 1632). This, for me, was not very impressive. I was eager to be baptized with water. I know I experienced the baptism of the Holy Spirit at regeneration and conversion, but as a Christian, I wanted to be baptized with water as the Lord Jesus had commanded. It was a great day when I could testify to the message in the old hymn which the congregation sang, "O happy day that fixed my choice on Thee, my Saviour and my God!"

After my baptism, I began to build up a library of good books for Bible study. The Bible, with my books as tools, I began to study earnestly. Very early in my Christian life I also became active in young people's Bible meetings. It was not long until I was also teaching a Sunday-school class. During World War I, I got my call to military service, but being a conscientious objector, I was never called to serve as a soldier.

By the time the war was over I felt the need for more intensive training and study. One day I told my parents (later my parents had changed their membership from their former affiliation to the Mennonite Church at St. Jacobs) that I had a conviction to go to our church school at Hesston, Kansas. It was not easy for my parents and brother and sister to give their approval, but they said, "Go and the Lord bless you." The Lord made it possible for me to finish my high school and two years of college work at Hesston and Goshen colleges. I had always hoped to become a missionary doctor, but like many other students I had to quit college when I was a junior, hoping to return later.

This was the turning point in the Lord's direction for my future service in the church. The first year that I was out of school, at the annual church conference at Markham, Ontario, two of the bishops had an interview with me, requesting me to assist a pastor who was sick. The Holy Spirit made it clear to me that my future service would be in the ministry and not as a missionary.

God in His grace has used me rather widely in the work of the church, in ways which in my early ministry I would have said were not possible. I had the joy of teaching in the Ontario Mennonite Bible School and Institute for thirty years, and for fifteen years the Lord used me as moderator of the Mennonite Conference of Ontario. I was appointed on many committees, occasionally served as evangelist in series of meetings, and as a teacher in Bible conferences. Another rich experience for me was serving for many years on the Executive Committee of the Mennonite Board of Missions and Charities. In Mennonite General Conference it was a joy to fellowship with brethren on different committees and to serve one term as moderator. In my service I can testify to the truth of Philippians 4:19: "But my God shall supply all your need according to his riches in glory."

18
The Lord Led Me

A. J. METZLER

One of the most gratifying things in my Christian experience has been to look back and see how the Lord has marvelously overruled and led in various ways in my Christian life and service, and especially how these have combined to prepare me step by step for the later chapters in my life.

The incidents relating to my decision to accept Christ as Saviour shall always remain vivid in my mind. My father was one of the ministers in a small congregation in central Pennsylvania. He was an evangelist and Bible teacher, and was frequently away from home in the work of the church. However, we were always aware of his keen interest in our welfare, and particularly of his spiritual concern for his family of eight children of which I was next to the youngest. At the age of eleven, when the usual annual revival meetings were held at our church, I was deeply under conviction as the Holy Spirit spoke to me of sin, and pressed the claims of Christ upon me. A number of others made the decision for Christ during those meetings, but I put it off.

The months that followed, during which I was keenly aware of my personal responsibilities to God, were a time of misery. I was afraid of everything. This simply meant that I feared the possibility of death, knowing that I was unprepared to meet God. The

---

A. J. Metzler was for over a quarter century the Publishing Agent, Herald Press (Mennonite Publishing House), Scottdale, Pennsylvania. He has also been widely used in evangelistic meetings and Bible conferences. Currently he is Executive Secretary of Mennonite General Conference.

following incident is typical of a number of experiences during those months of distress. One hot summer evening my younger brother and I retired early, as rural folks did in those days. A heavy thunderstorm developed, with lightning and thunder unusually strong. In my terrible fear I imagined lightning would strike the house at any time, and if it did so, resulting in my death, I knew that I was doomed! Father and Mother's bedroom was on the first floor. Father was away. I slipped out of my upstairs bed, went quietly down the stairs, through the living room and dining room, into Mother's bedroom, and crawled under her bed.

Why did I do this? Normally I had paid little attention to thunderstorms. But I was afraid—terrible fear gripped my heart. It made me a coward, simply because God had called, and I had not responded. I knew that I was not ready to meet Him.

My wise father, of course, sensed the struggle through which I was going at this period in my life. I shall always remember that morning, as I was helping with the chores at the stable, when Father laid his hand upon my shoulder. He asked me if I did not want to accept Christ as my Saviour, and very simply he explained what it would mean. I was so glad for his personal approach, and right there I made my decision, and told Father so. There were glad people in that stable. The burden rolled from my heart, and from that day on there was a freedom, liberty, and joy not known before. This was the time and place of my decision for Christ, and the great experience of the new birth.

One way in which God has continued to reveal Himself more clearly is through sudden flashes and insights as to the meaning of various Scripture which the Holy Spirit has been pleased to give me. I remember vividly, for example, one incident many years ago. It was in the late 1920's, and I was en route to Eastern Mennonite College for a Christian Life Conference. Having a couple hours' layover between bus and train in Cumberland, Maryland, I went to a restaurant for lunch and part of the waiting time. I was reading in Ephesians when verse four of chapter one opened up to me in a clearer way than ever before. It reads, "According as he hath chosen us in him before the foundation of the world. . . ." What a tremendous blessing came to me when I suddenly realized that I was not just an afterthought with God! For Him I was not just a recent idea, someone that He first noticed as a lad when His Spirit called me to accept Christ. Not by any means. He chose me personally to be in Christ before the foundation of the world. It was He who created the world in the beginning. That immediately takes us beyond the powers of our mind to grasp or comprehend. This goes back untold millenniums—how long before any recorded history, we do not know; but God did not choose me at the time of the creation. It was at the beginning of the beginning, because the foundation (in the figure of a house) is the first thing in the construction. Here again we are far, far back beyond anything our imagination is able to comprehend. We note further that it was not only at the beginning of the beginning (that is, at the time of foundation laying), but "before the foundation." In other words, it was *before* the beginning of the beginning. That is the time when God chose me to be in Christ. To think that God looked down through eternity, if that is the proper figure, through all of time, and saw me and chose me to be in Christ!

My place in the thought and affection of God, my place as a member of the body of Christ, goes back then to the dim eternity of the past, and by His grace my place in Christ goes on into the glorious eternity of the future. We can only stand in awe, and borrow the words of the Apostle Paul in Romans: "What shall we then say to these things? If God be for us, who can be against us?" And God is for us, He has been for us, through all the millenniums of past time, and before that. He will be for us in the eternity of the future. "What shall we then say to these things?" *Nothing but praise!* For it has all been said, and far more has been said than we could possibly comprehend. Again the words of Paul become ours: "O the depth of the riches both of the wisdom and knowledge of God! how unsearchable are his judgments, and his ways past finding out" (Romans 11:33)!

On September 24, 1922, at nineteen years of age, I went to work for the C. H. Musselman Company as a foreman in charge of about one hundred and twenty-five men and women in a department of what was then the largest apple-processing plant in this country. I had never seen a wheel turn in a canning plant before that Monday morning when the plant began operations for the season. I never did know whether their choice in putting an inexperienced young man into this position was simply a gambling chance, or whether the fact that the president of the company and my father were neighbor boys on adjoining farms in Lancaster County years before contributed to my being given that opportunity! At any rate, the work was most fascinating, and apparently I took the responsibility seriously. A month later when some former school friends visited the plant, and I had shown them through it, one of the ladies responsible to me said, "Mr. Metzler, we never knew that you could smile until today."

Various responsibilities were added in the course of time and the work appealed to me so much that I enrolled for a course in Industrial Management with the La Salle Extension University of Chicago. To pursue these studies late at night, and then to apply what I was learning on the job, added interest both to my studies and to my work. Sixteen months later, on January 1, 1924, when I had just passed my twenty-first birthday anniversary, I was made superintendent of the entire operations. The challenge and fascinations of the work increased with the added responsibility. However, another major milestone came on November 16 of the same year, 1924, when my home congregation at Martinsburg, Pennsylvania, ordained me and another brother to the ministry. When I announced to my employer and my friends my intentions of resigning to enter the ministry, there was quite a protest, and much "friendly" counsel was given. To many of them it seemed foolish indeed for a young man who had such promising opportunities for advancement in the business world to make such a move. The president of the company spent considerable time with me trying to show the opportunities I had where I was. In the light of further advancements he had scheduled for me, I could share among other things in building up a substantial foundation which he anticipated would keep fifty young men perpetually in training for the ministry. This, he thought, would be a much greater opportunity than my going into the ministry myself.

However, it seemed to me to be a perfectly clear call of God through the church, and I never questioned it for a moment, nor was I tempted to consider at all the attractive proposition given me. However, I did want to be fair with the firm which had given me such opportunities, and therefore I gave them one year to find my successor. Thus, at the end of the season, the latter part of 1925, I left to join the ministers of the small congregation at Martinsburg, and secured a job as a common laborer, sweeping floors in a railroad shop in Altoona, Pennsylvania.

These years, 1924 and 1925, had been significant ones for me. In April of 1924 my beloved father had passed away. On May 16, 1924, I was married to Alta Maust of Springs, Pennsylvania. My ordination to the ministry occurred in November, 1924, and in February, 1925, the first of our six children was born. During 1926 the Southwestern Pennsylvania (now Allegheny) Conference, and the congregation at Masontown, invited me to serve at Masontown as pastor. We located there in November, 1926, after a year's employment at the railroad shop, and part-time pastoral services at the small congregation of Schellsburg in Bedford County, to which we had traveled every two weeks the forty miles from Martinsburg.

The work at Masontown greatly interested us. We were completely inexperienced at pastoral work, and as we took up the services in the congregation of sixty-three members, with an attendance in Sunday school of about fifty, we soon saw tremendous need, not only in the congregation, but in that whole mining community of southwestern Pennsylvania. The Lord's blessing rested upon the work, the congregation was co-operative and responsive, and in nearly ten years the congregational membership doubled, and the Sunday-school attendance nearly tripled.

During this time my opportunities for service and experience in the church widened. I had five or six series of revival meetings each year and had opportunity to serve on various committees and boards, such as sharing in the work of the General Sunday School Committee, being chairman of the district Sunday School Conference, and other similar responsibilities. I had no idea during these years in business, in pastoral and general church work, what the Lord was getting me ready for. I cannot recall thinking ahead beyond the many opportunities at hand.

However, in June, 1935, when I was invited to accept the office of General Manager of the Mennonite Publishing House, Scottdale, Pennsylvania, the whole pattern began to come clear. When I received the call from the Mennonite Publication Board, and began to see some of the requirements for the job, I could clearly see the Lord's hand in giving me the few years' experience as an administrator in business, as well as His leading me to take a course in Industrial Engineering. Furthermore, I could see His hand in the ten years of pastoral experience, and in getting acquainted with the work of the church at the grass roots, as well as with the church at large in Bible conferences and evangelistic meetings, and in serving on district conference and general church committees. The opportunities in those thirteen years were a training course specifically preparing me for my contribution to the denominational literature program for the twenty-eight years as Publishing House administrator which then lay ahead.

The call to serve as Executive Secretary of Mennonite General Conference was another clear indication of the Lord's leading, somewhat similar to the earlier call, but of course different in many details. There was the long preparation in all levels of church work, and in a variety of phases of each—congregational, district conference, and general church program. It has been my privilege to be a member of the three major boards of the church (Education, Publication, Missions), and to serve as officer or administrator in one capacity or another in all three of them. I had worked closely with most of the institutions of the church, as well as with the various general committees. It was my privilege to share in the committee that for four years (1933-37) studied and revamped the Christian education organization, bringing various agencies into the newly formed Commission for Christian Education. I became chairman of the Commission, and was later secretary-treasurer of it for many years. In a similar way I had the privilege of sharing in the eleven-man committee which spent a number of years in the 1940's making a study of our general conference organization, and proposing to General Conference the plan which was accepted and has now been in operation for about fifteen years. All of this has given me an opportunity to become acquainted with our entire brotherhood, including the district conferences and most of their leaders, and General Conference and its various institutions and organizations. I could not well decline the invitation to accept the executive secretaryship of the brotherhood in 1961.

Truly, the Lord doth move in mysterious ways His wonders to perform. His many promises to lead have been abundantly confirmed over and over again.

19
A Gradual Awakening

IVAN J. MILLER

*"The lines are fallen unto me in pleasant places;
yea, I have a goodly heritage" (Psalm 16:6).*

On May 7, 1911, near Grantsville, Maryland, a son was born to Jonas B. and Barbara Swartzentruber Miller. He was the ninth child in their family of four sons and seven daughters, and was named Ivan. The family was reared on a modest farm homestead one-half mile north of Grantsville. Father was a minister in the Casselman River Conservative Mennonite Church. As the children grew to maturity, they all became Christians, and united with the church where their father served.

The children were heirs to a rich family heritage which they were early taught to respect. The known Miller line of descent is as follows: (1) John, who came to the community from eastern Pennsylvania with his sons in the latter part of the eighteenth century; (2) Jacob, who secured his land from the state of Pennsylvania in 1783, and who was ordained to the ministry of the Amish Mennonite Church in the Somerset County, Pennsylvania-Garrett County, Maryland, area, later moving to Ohio; (3) Benedict, probably the first Amish Mennonite bishop to be ordained in the Grantsville area, and influential in church work beyond his native state; (4) Joel B., a community figure whose craftsmanship produced furniture, spinning wheels, tools, and other items, stamped

---

Ivan J. Miller is pastor and bishop of the Maple Glen congregation, Grantsville, Maryland, and a leader in the Conservative Mennonite Conference.

with his name and date and even yet abounding in the community; (5) Joel J., Amish Mennonite bishop who carried the burden of church leadership at a time when differences were disturbing the peace in the Somerset County-Garrett County area, and who reluctantly led his charge on a more progressive course that others could follow, thus becoming an early bishop in the Conservative Mennonite Church; (6) Jonas B., widely known minister in the Conservative Mennonite Conference, and long-time English editor of the periodical, *Herold der Wahrheit*.

Mother was Barbara, a granddaughter of Christian and Barbara Bender Swartzentruber, who came to America from Germany in 1837. Her parents were Jacob and Elizabeth Hershberger Swartzentruber, who lived at Redhouse on the Northwestern Turnpike, now U.S. Highway 50, during Civil War days. Here they suffered crippling financial reverses through loss of their livestock at the hand of raiding parties, both of the Northern and Southern armies.

Though family history was often discussed with appreciation, Father was also aware of current issues and trends in the church, for he was an avid reader, and had a surprising grasp of trends throughout the churches, including other denominations. Sometimes he agreed with these trends and sometimes he was not in agreement. Usually his reactions were honest and vigorous. His preaching and writing were forthright and to the point. Sometimes he was almost stern and unyielding. In church and family life he demonstrated unswerving integrity. In the pulpit, Father was an orator. His audiences were moved by the emotions he felt as he preached.

Mother was a quiet, unassuming woman, devoted to Father, and self-sacrificially given to mothering their children. Her calmness and quiet endurance seemed to me to have been the perfect balance to Father's nervous energy and drive.

Around these two persons my childhood world revolved. My first knowledge of God came through them, as did also my first impressions of right and wrong. When my childish mind was just beginning to grasp some of the realities of life, Grandfather Miller died. I was four years of age. As the congregation met in the funeral service of their bishop, I noticed for the first time in my life that adults could weep. This was disturbing to me. I was further disturbed when I gazed at Grandfather's lifeless body. Why did he appear so different? And what would become of his body, lowered into the grave and covered with earth? Would we never see him again?

The evening after the funeral I took these perplexing problems to Mother. From her I received simple and satisfying answers which began to formulate some of the basic beliefs which constitute my faith today. And so at the age of four I was told what all children should learn—grief and sorrow do bring weeping and tears, but the hope of a Christian will never leave him in frustration and despair. Death had come near, but not inside our immediate home. Life continued for the family without serious disruption. The goodness of God was everywhere around us. Spring with its maple sugar-making and seeding was followed by summer with its haying and strawberry harvesting. Fall with its harvesting was followed by winter with its snows and storms. The family income was very limited, but the children always felt the security of home ties and parental protection.

During these happy years I was privileged to attend a good country school. Yoder school had one room with rows of stationary desks, a potbellied stove, a two-gallon water fountain filled from the neighbor's spring, and other comparable equipment. But the community was awake, and the school was considered one of the better one-room schools in the county. By the time I "graduated" from Yoder we had two rooms, heating, plumbing, and lighting facilities. This came about through the interest and effort of the local community. I completed the seventh grade when thirteen years of age. Here my formal education terminated. My lack of education continues to be one of my constant regrets. The local high schools were not thought safe to attend. Our church at that time frowned on higher education. My parents could not advance finances to educate all of their large family, and so circumstances combined to deny me the learning I often longed for. Today I feel no resentment against anyone because of this. I am sure that our church and my parents held their views on formal

115

training in all sincerity. I am only sorry that I am thus limited.

In the spring of 1923, when I was eleven, the first great sorrow entered our home. Mother became ill with pneumonia. At her request Bishop C. W. Bender anointed her with oil in the presence of the family. The next days her life seemed to hang by a mere thread. One afternoon she requested that the family sing to her the hymns, "How Firm a Foundation" and "I Need Thee Every Hour." Then she had Father call the children into the room one by one to say good-by. Her last admonition to me I shall never forget, "Be faithful and sometime you also shall come where I am going." The next morning she had gone to be with her Lord.

The next days seemed much like a confused dream to me. Friends came and went. They spoke words of comfort and offered help, but it seemed to my boyish heart nothing could help. Life's pattern seemed to have fallen into utter confusion. Yet several things stood out which strengthened me. Christian hope showed through the cloud. In conversations, in Scripture readings, in prayers, in the funeral service—all around me the hope of eternal life was emphasized. The morning after the funeral, Father in his strong voice led the family in prayer for the future with such courage and deep devotion, coupled with hope and faith, that I found myself reaching out to God in childlike trust.

This experience caused me to do some earnest soul-searching. Now, almost twelve years old, I began to think through some problems for myself. For the first time, life appeared to be a personal responsibility. No longer could my elders make all my decisions for me. When Mother's illness became critical, and finally death came, my boyish heart almost rebelled against God. We needed her so much. Why did God permit this? Did God really care for us? These and other questions pressed on my maturing mind. I was rapidly approaching the place where my life would become centered in self, or by a conscious decision of mind centered on God. *I met God.*

During the months after Mother's funeral there were times of lonely despair, interspersed with times of courage. Gently, firmly, God was speaking to me. After all, God's grace and goodness were still surrounding us. Life had a purpose, and life had a meaning.

But both the purpose and the meaning of life would be defeated without God. Over an extended period of time my childhood trust in God, largely depending on the teaching of others, was being replaced by a personal faith which would be my very life. I was experiencing the new birth. It came, not in an instantaneous climactic experience, but rather as a gradual awakening. During the summer of 1925 I joined a class of converts, at the invitation of our bishop, and after a series of instruction, mostly from the Dordrecht Confession of Faith, we were baptized in the fall.

During these first years of my Christian life, more intimate counsel and help than I received would have been appreciated. Likewise, during my late teens, confidential counsel and warning concerning dangers of personal and social life would have been of great benefit. During these years my faith held firm, but in practical living I knew the heartache and guilt of yielding to sin. Yet God was always near and ready to forgive.

As I grew to manhood, the Lord led me to a life companion whose influence has done more to shape my life than any other person. Della is the daughter of the late Bishop Christian W. and Ida Hershberger Bender. Reared in the home of an active, influential church leader, her outlook on life was similar to mine; we discovered this early in our friendship. We were married on May 28, 1931, by her father. Since then, we have enjoyed the most intimate fellowship through varied experiences. What little I have been able to do for the Lord, by His grace has been largely due to her wise counsel and energetic support. Often her clear vision and optimism have pointed the way to workable conclusions which would have been most difficult for me to come to alone. We were blessed with three sons and six daughters. All but the two youngest, who are yet immature children, have embraced the Christian faith. To see our children grow into useful servants of Christ is one of our chief delights.

On June 19, 1938, I was ordained to the ministry in the home congregation by my father-in-law, C. W. Bender. In my role as a young minister, I received many blessings through my acquaintance with faithful and able ministers who were my seniors, as well as zealous men of my own age. Divine purpose and direction became reality. But after serving in the ministry for twelve years, one of the most staggering temptations of my entire life struck. A certain difficulty was straining brotherly relations in the congregation. Brethren whom I loved and respected did not understand each other. In the ensuing confusion my own peace was disturbed. The subtle temptation came to me to doubt the reality of my Christian faith. For several days this persisted with increasing vehemence. I began to doubt the very existence of God. If the church and fellow Christians who professed faith in Christ could not discern the will of God, and show love to each other, how could I know that there is a God? The conflict within me built up to a climactic storm of doubt and uncertainty that shook my very soul. Satan was trying to overthrow my faith. For several hours one afternoon the battle raged. And then, in answer to my earnest and continued prayer for deliverance, the tempter left, and peace and assurance again became my possession.

This experience, I believe, was one of the most outstanding steppingstones in my life. The faithfulness of the Father, the Saviour's words of peace and assurance, the power of the Holy Spirit, the direct and immediate answer to my prayer for deliverance from doubt—all this confirmed my faith, and convinces me to this day that no testing of faith can ever defeat us if we humbly stay close to God.

On October 1, 1953, I was ordained to the office of bishop. The opportunities thus afforded to serve Christ in His church have brought a wealth of blessings.

Now fifty years of age, thirty-seven years a Christian, twenty-four years a minister, what does my heavenly Father want to teach me today? "Christ liveth in me," Paul wrote in Galatians 2:20. This I would strive for: death to self, life in Christ, a dynamic faith, a Christlikeness that draws others to Him, not to men or to systems, but to His own blessed person.

20
What Christ Has Meant to Me

PAUL MININGER

I first met Jesus Christ when I was facing the problem of moral failure. Although I was but a young boy, I felt ashamed and guilty for certain things I had done. At this early date I learned that because of Jesus Christ and His death I had the promise of forgiveness and acceptance with God.

Christ met me again during my high-school days. Another moral problem brought the words of Romans 7 home to me: "I do not do what I want, but I do the very thing I hate" (RSV). This was clearly my experience. It made me think of the time when I learned to ride a bicycle. Whenever I would try hard not to hit some stone or obstacle in my way, I would hit it every time. So it is in the struggle against sin. I learned that Jesus Christ, and not self-effort, is the answer to sin and temptation.

Jesus met me again during my college career. Four of us were traveling from Newton to Hesston, Kansas, in a Model T Ford, when another car hit us from the side. Although thrown quite a distance from the car, I got up and walked back. The other boys said that I was hurt, and took me to a doctor. After he had sewed me up, he said, "Had this cut been just a little deeper, it would have cut the jugular vein." Life had been in the balances, and this is a pretty severe shock for a college boy.

In this crisis two things happened. First, I discovered that

Paul Mininger is a minister and bishop, and a leader in the Mennonite Church. Since 1954 he has served as president of Goshen College.

Christ can remove the fear of death. Second, I began to ask what I should do with my life. In the providence of God, my life had been spared, and I began to wonder why. Was there some reason for this? I determined to live my life so as to carry out the purposes of Christ. Since He is working out these purposes in the church, I understood this to mean an identification with the program and mission of the church.

Christ has met me many times since then, especially in times of moral and ethical decision. In the midst of the complexities and difficulties of knowing right from wrong, Christ has led me. He has enabled me to make decisions where otherwise there would have been only bewilderment and despair.

Christ has also met me and has been with me in the midst of what few difficulties and major problems I have had. I have probably had less than my share of suffering and testing. To be sure, there have been doubts and disappointments; there have been responsibilities and frustration, and a few discouragements. But I have probably had less than my share of these. However, in the midst of those which I have had, Christ has been a living presence. His grace has always been sufficient.

As I have grown in years and in Christian experience, Jesus Christ has become increasingly significant for me in all aspects of life. I must say that life for me has not been a vale of tears. It has not been a great burden; really, I have had a rich and full life, and the gifts of God have been many. The goodness of God has, in fact, called me to repentance more often than have the difficulties and disciplines of life. I have enjoyed the love of a very wonderful family, and the companionship of many friends. I have enjoyed pleasant work and good colleagues to work with. I have had the opportunity for study and reflection, and during the years of my preparation, considerable leisure to think and to study and to live. These gifts have had meaning for me in proportion to my dedication to Jesus Christ.

Finally, Christ has also helped me in my search for freedom. I am a human being, and like others, I have sought freedom. I have found true freedom, but only because I have learned that freedom in itself is meaningless. Freedom has meaning only in relationship to an individual's purpose in life. One needs freedom to achieve his goal. And Christ gives us this freedom when we dedicate ourselves to Him.

(Condensed from a chapel talk given at Goshen College, Goshen, Indiana.)

21
Seeing an Accident as God's Mercy

MELVIN MOYER, as told to H. C. Wenger

On August 5, 1950, I was a thirty-year-old farmer living near Blooming Glen, Pennsylvania, with a Christian wife and two children. I was a very ungodly man, refusing to pray to God, and also refusing to accompany my wife to church.

Soon after lunch on that fateful August day something jammed in my hay baler. With the tractor motor running wide open I jumped off the tractor and hurried back to the baler. I had dirt in my eyes from the dust. Noticing that the binder twine was not feeding properly into the baler, I tried to feed it in by hand. To this day I do not know exactly what happened, but suddenly my arm was jerked violently into the rollers of the baler with such force that the tractor almost stalled. It was only the fact that it was running wide open which enabled the motor to keep going. I was pulled into the rollers clear up to my head and body. The rollers began grinding away at my arm and shoulder. I had one time seen a fence post go through the baler and come out all smashed to pieces, and I expected the same thing to happen to me. At any moment I expected to be drawn completely into the baler and crushed to death.

It seems, however, that I was wedged in in such a fashion that the rollers did not pull me any farther into the baler, but kept grinding away on my right shoulder and arm. The belt also was rubbing and slapping me in the face until my face, nose, and eyes

---

Melvin Moyer, a Pennsylvania farmer, is a member of the Blooming Glen Mennonite Church.

were lacerated and bleeding. Indeed, the doctors who later treated me thought that I would lose my left eye. In my plight I was not able to see, but I did remain conscious. The friction of the rollers grinding and slipping on my shoulder generated so much heat that the flesh looked as though it had been burned. (The hay in the baler and around the front of the baler was burned from the heat of the friction of the stalled baler.) My clothing also was torn and burned. The heat cauterized the large blood vessels in my shoulder and arm so that I did not bleed to death.

I called and called for help, but no one heard me. Finally, I began to pray. I had never prayed before, but had always laughed at God, and at the idea of prayer. I had always thought that prayer was complete foolishness.

Every Sunday morning when my dear wife left for church she told me that she would be praying for me, asking God to change my life. I just laughed at her. She had recently told me that she asked God to let something happen that would change me. But so completely had Satan taken hold of me that I was thinking of separating from my wife and getting a divorce. On her part she did everything she could to bring me to Christ. She had asked me to permit her to ask the minister to come and talk to me and explain the way of salvation to me. I had refused.

But now I prayed. I begged God to save me from going through the baler. I promised Him to change my life if only He would help me now. At first, I did not feel as though God had heard me. I also called loudly for human help. Finally I began getting so weak that I could hardly call at all. I had just about given up when suddenly God spoke to me. He asked me whether I was not going to swear now. I said, "No, because this is my last day on earth." (Indeed, I was able to see right into hell.) God assured me that He would spare my life if I would change my way of living. I, however, felt that I was not able to make any such change. In any case, God said, "Call once more and someone will hear you." Actually I did not believe this, but finally I called, not very loud, for I was already too weak. Strange as it may seem, a neighbor appeared immediately and stopped the tractor. I knew that this man had a heart condition, and I told him not to get excited, but to go and call the implement dealer to come and get me out. I had already been in the baler about one hour. The dealer could not be located.

The neighbor then called the ambulance. The men in the ambulance, however, were unable to free me; so they in turn called the fire company. About fifty men responded. They got to work with the wheel, cut the belts, and pried the rollers apart, and finally succeeded in freeing me.

My shoulder and arm were almost ground off. I was taken by ambulance to the Grand View Hospital, where the doctors felt there was nothing to do, for they believed that I would soon die. However, the Lord had spoken to me and assured me that He was going to restore me and give me another opportunity to witness for Him. In any case a team of four doctors operated, removing my torn and mangled flesh and cleaning out the dirt from the wounds as best they could.

Early Sunday morning I awoke, but at that time did not remember anything about the accident. My wife was sitting beside my bed and she explained that I was in the hospital and that I had lost my arm (actually I had lost both arm and shoulder). On Sunday I prayed and I worried. How could I drive a car? How could I do my farming? My good wife tried to encourage me. Best of all, God spoke to me again and assured me that I would be able to do everything which I had done before.

My wife came to the decision that it would be best to remove me to the University of Pennsylvania Hospital, thirty miles away in Philadelphia. At first I objected, but finally I agreed when I felt assured that this move was within the will of God. So on Thursday morning, five days after the accident, against the wishes of the local physicians, who believed that the trip would kill me, I was taken by ambulance to Philadelphia. After the doctors there had seen me, they told my wife that they had no hopes for my life, but that they would do whatever they could. They operated immediately and tried to repair and thoroughly clean my wounded body. They grafted skin to cover the area which had been most severely injured. They also gave me large amounts of blood. Both my wife and I prayed earnestly, as also did our friends.

My appetite then became enormous. I ate anything and everything which they brought to me. The doctors and nurses were both amazed and pleased at the way I ate and gained strength. Three weeks after my admission to the University Hospital I was taken home. The doctors regarded it as a miracle.

By the end of October I was again on my tractor planting wheat. Some time later, I decided that it was now time to begin to do my own milking again. You will remember that God had promised me that I would be able to do everything I had done before. Nevertheless, every time I tried to fasten the milker on a cow it would drop for me and get all dirty. I tried and tried, and finally felt completely defeated, so much so that I went to the house and wept. I then prayed and asked God to help me afresh. Again my brave wife encouraged me. I then went out to the barn, and put the milker on the cows all by myself. I have a large herd of Holstein cattle.

Yes, it was a terrible tragedy to lose my arm and shoulder, and yet if I had the choice between being restored as I was before the accident, living the way I lived then, and being handicapped as I am now, but a child of God, I would gladly remain as I am. I would rather have one arm and be a child of God than have two good arms and be a lost sinner. I am so thankful that God allowed me to be injured in order to bring me to repentance and faith. I know that He answers prayer because He answered my prayers and those of my friends, especially of my wife, for my salvation. God has been good to us and given us five additional children since the time of this accident. It has been my privilege to give my witness as to what God has done for me before the entire Blooming Glen congregation, and it is my desire that I may ever witness for my Saviour as He gives me opportunity.

(See also the article, "One Hour Made All the Difference," by Irene L. Bishop, in *Christian Living,* October, 1962, page 28.)

22
From Rebellion to Discipleship

JOHN R. MUMAW

I was born in a Christian home, being one of eleven children. My father was a minister of the Gospel and my mother was a faithful "shepherdess" serving the cause of Christ in modesty and subordination. Grief clouded the family scene when during my mother's recuperation from serious illness death took away my father. It left my mother with her family, with a mortgage, and with a vital faith. The farm operations went on, the children grew, and church activities were always given high priority. The family altar in the home was continued with regularity and devotion. It provided a good climate in which to face encounter with God.

I was the youngest child. Church, school, and community all provided opportunity to form many friendships and to absorb a moderate culture. I encountered a mixture of influences ranging from the results of alcoholic indulgence to the values of strict religious standards. In the midst of all the good and bad, a prevailing resentment emerged. I felt I had been cheated in life through being deprived of a father's indulgence and understanding. What I saw among my playmates, who often referred to "Papa," created an attitude that made me vulnerable to evil influences. The ways of the world had sensual attractions and the life of the church lost its meaning for me. There were moments of desire for good, stimulated by good people in my company, including my own family.

John R. Mumaw is a minister and leader in his denomination, and president of Eastern Mennonite College, Harrisonburg, Virginia.

One Christmas morning my older brothers and sisters were sitting in the living room talking casually about significant Christian experiences. Their own lives had been good evidence to me of the reality of Christian faith. I had deep longings for the kind of satisfaction they had demonstrated to me without their knowing it. I could have been led to Christ at that moment if they had known the real openness of my heart. Instead, I went to the barn alone and wore down the edge of conviction born in that family fellowship.

Outside the family there were people of evil inclination, especially among my peers, who contributed to my tendency toward evil. Circumstances in the community during World War I confused my status, for I was counted with the "rejected" CO's while I was counting myself with the world. I had feelings of sympathy for a CO brother being mistreated by army officials, while at the same time I was entertaining thoughts of gaining popularity in a sensate society. As a teen-ager growing up with these inner tensions and social conflicts I was about to abandon faith and its moral restraints for worldly ambitions and sensual indulgence.

The World War closed, but my inner soul struggle persisted. Community tensions subsided, but my conflict of ambitions increased. Desire for an education prevailed, but the conditions for securing it were frustrating. I was given the choice of terminating my schooling with two years of high school or attending a church school. In the course of several days in which I had to make my decision I felt a threat against my worldly ambitions, my habits of indulgence, and the hope of popular success. What was even more disturbing was the rumor that students at E.M.C. "get converted." And of course it seemed clear to me that my mother could not afford to spend that much money! But rather than lose my chance to keep on going to school I decided to "endure" two years of religious pressures in order to secure a high-school diploma.

Dormitory life was a new experience. I was assigned a "good" fellow for my roommate. Thoughts went through my mind during the first week that made me consider the advantages of being like this Christian. Others of my classmates too seemed to enjoy prayer circle, chapel, decent conversations in the dining hall, clean speech on the athletic field, and a jolly good time in the off-hours of school. During this first week I began to think it would not be too bad after all to fit in with this crowd if I could only feel and think as they did. But one walk to town (a mile away) with a fellow student canceled that with one sentence of conversation. He had appeared to me as being one of the foremost leaders in conversation on religious topics. I was a bit suspicious about his inviting me to go with him on this occasion. "How can I be good enough for him?" I thought. But out of courtesy I agreed to go. We were hardly off campus when the bubble burst. In answer to a question he replied with the reinforcement of cursing. I was amazed! He had impressed me with a piety that I would never have dared to invade with vulgarity. But now the old lines of communication were opened again and I got temporary release in the free exchange of words on a sinner's level. Having found a "fellow fool" I lost the faint desires for reform.

Of course this kind of "community" had to go underground. We knew very well it would not be tolerated on the campus. A few others spilled their folly into our company. The "gang" formed a code of behavior and a method of operation that eluded attempts to uncover our sins. Fall revival meetings made little impression on me, even in the face of evident change in the lives of some students. Special prayer groups were reported, but such formalities made little difference to me. Life was too full of fun to turn toward serious prayer and piety. Why should I give up my free ambitions for a strait jacket in religion? And so time wore on until midyear revival meetings, with John S. Mast preaching morning and evening.

The revival had reached a point of deep concern. Great souls prayed for victory. Personal workers were witnessing. The preaching was getting stronger and the fires of revival were getting warmer, but very little happened. Few people responded. I was getting a bit uneasy, fearing I might be called in for an interview. I figured that I might be able to evade that ordeal if I should pretend (how awful the thought!) penitence and make a "confession" by responding publicly to the evangelist's invitation to stand. This I did (to my shame). This precipitated a "break" in the meetings and a tremendous wave of conviction swept through that audience. Scores of people responded until over one hundred had stood in acknowledgment of their sins. This so deeply impressed me that I was moved to get up again, this time in honest confession. But I stifled conviction and rejected the call to repentance.

Several weeks later my absence from the campus was covered by the surveillance of the principal, J. B. Smith. He established beyond any doubt in his mind and mine that I was guilty of misdemeanor and transgression of school regulations. While returning to the campus my resolution was made. If the restrictions should be made so much as a "campus," I would disappear and find the road that would lead to my worldly ambitions.

That evening I was called from my room to appear before the faculty. On my way I had a private vision of destiny. The end of a sinner's road looked horrible indeed. The whole ordeal was taking on serious proportions. The interview was conducted with kindness. My teachers were moved with evident compassion. Their prayers were by all the marks of my judgment genuine. I was the object of real concern. I was guilty! I was sorry! I promised to make a public statement in chapel the next morning. The case was dismissed. I never found out what followed in that meeting, but I know what happened in my room.

Upon my return to the dormitory I went immediately to my room and without saying a word to my roommate fell to my knees by the bed and poured out my soul in silent but deep contrition before God. After pleading for pardon I claimed the promise of forgiveness and found real peace. I have never doubted the reality of that experience and have since then had assurance of my salvation through faith in the risen and redeeming Christ.

This experience of saving grace remains a constant reminder of my debt to God for all He did for me then and since. It turned the course of my life into paths of peace and ways of pleasantness. For this I am profoundly grateful, for in God's grace I have been blessed with a happy home, with opportunities for service in the Mennonite Church, and with the challenge of a stimulating vocation. I know that I am totally unworthy of it all; so I seek to glorify Him always in the dedication of my life to Christian service.

23
A Moralist's Pilgrimage

JOHN S. OYER

I began life as a "good boy." All hands admit it! Even my oldest sister, who has the most fabulous memory in our family, admits it. She thought that I was disgustingly good. I was guilty of a few peccadilloes, but no grave sins. This goodness was a kind of scrupulousness. I was scrupulous about everything. I mention this because it is a source of a very significant problem that I did not realize as a problem until considerably later in my life, and also because I think quite a few Mennonites face this problem. It is part of our tradition. Relative goodness can be in itself a serious spiritual problem—a block to the realization of one's need for Christ. My problem was: How can a "good boy" become a Christian? I began to recognize this problem especially in my study of Paul, and still later in reading Luther.

When I was a boy, Christianity meant my congregation, and only slightly more, the Mennonite Church. I developed a very negative attitude toward Mennonitism. It was itself too negative. It was principally a denial of the things I wanted to do. I remember very little of this bleak period in my life except that I determined I was not going to marry a Mennonite. Mennonites were much too tame. (My religious awakening or discovery went hand in glove with the discovery of the relevance of Mennonitism.)

Our congregation held revival meetings annually, and these

John S. Oyer has studied at Harvard (A.M.), Chicago (Ph.D.), and Heidelberg universities, and is Associate Professor of History, Goshen College. He is married and is the father of three daughters and one son.

troubled me a great deal. I felt guilty because I had had no overwhelming spiritual experience which radically altered my way of life. It seemed to me that revival meetings called for such an experience. I developed the mistaken notion that God worked in men only through some dramatic Pauline experience. My failure in achieving such an experience troubled me off and on for years, until I was almost thirty years old. I was sure I was damned, because I had no faith—meaning a strongly emotional experience. I turned faith into a subjective experience and I prayed earnestly for one. I will return to this problem later.

I was drafted at the end of my freshman year in Goshen College. I spent three years as a registered conscientious objector in several Civilian Public Service camps, to be followed by three more years of relief work in Europe. These six years became the decisive turning period of my life. There were many influences which shaped me. For one thing, I began to change my evaluation of Mennonitism as being only negative. This actually began during my freshman year in college. I began to enjoy worship services. I enjoyed chapel singing, and also I enjoyed the Mennonite girls. I wrestled with the negative dimensions of conscientious objection to war. Did we only sit out the war? People said we did. In my first CPS camp, in the Shenandoah Valley of Virginia, we lived a few miles from the town of Grottoes. Whenever we drove through town on our way to the project, there was always someone walking along the street who would yell "CO's" or "yellow bellies" at us. We were made to feel very keenly that we were fourth-rate citizens. Since that time I have come to blame the American government for not giving us the opportunity of working at something more significant than soil conservation or forestry projects, or even mental hospital work. We were not permitted to enter foreign relief work, where there might have been physical danger. Selective Service was interested in drafting men for war service and they obviously were not out to popularize the CO position. They left us "stuck" in the United States, where we were accused of being "yellow bellies." But I discovered in CPS that many Mennonites were intensely sincere and earnest about their faith, and that they were also courageous.

It was a shock to move from the relative ignominy of CPS to relief work in Germany, where Lutheran pastors told their congregations that the American Mennonites were the best modern-day examples of Christians who demonstrated true Christian love. People turned in their pews to gaze at us; we felt like museum pieces. The Mennonite in the United States was a fourth-rate citizen; in Germany, in 1947, the American Mennonite was praised to the skies. (I learned also in my experience in Kiel and Hamburg, Germany, to deeply appreciate God's other, non-Mennonite sheep.) I am still filled with awe at how much the people of Kiel, a city of 350,000 inhabitants, respected and remembered Mennonites. In the summer of 1959 my family and I were visiting friends in Kiel on our way back to the United States. I had a used Volkswagen which I wanted to sell. I can still remember talking to a prospective buyer. In the course of our conversation he asked where I had learned the German language. When I told him that I had worked for two years in Kiel with the Mennonite Central Committee, his face lighted up immediately. From that time on he was perfectly willing to believe anything that I told him about the car. It put me on my guard to be very careful of my statements.

In relief work I also learned to marvel at the power of God working through men whose inadequacies were glaring, inadequacies which seemed to be more real than their Christian spirit. Our Mennonite Central Committee units were made up of people who sometimes quarreled over petty matters and who were concerned too much with matters of status. Yet some people found Christ through us. I found this to be a very humbling experience. Let me give you several illustrations. Heinrich was a student who left the University of Leipzig during the winter semester of 1948-49 and came to Hamburg. He left Leipzig and fled to West Germany because, as one of twelve members of the Student Council at the university, he refused to kowtow to increasing pressure from the communist authorities. He left his family in the Russian zone. He was painfully conscious of their exposure to communist pressures because of his own flight. He recommenced the study of law at the University of Hamburg, and he happened to be included in a group of students who were invited to our center. We had many experiences with people who came to our center partly, or largely, because we had food and clothing, and these things were in short supply, to say the least, in Germany at that time. We learned in the course of a few months' experience how to detect those people who came to us for material benefits. Heinrich was not one of them. When he returned repeatedly to visit, I asked him why he came. Surely it was not our intellectual attainments which drew him in; in the midst of German students we always felt culturally inferior, because we were. Heinrich told me he came to us because he found in us a light which he had never seen anywhere before. Really? How could the light of Christ emanate from us, with all our bickering? I learned to my astonishment how God works with power through the very inadequate human resources at His disposal.

As another example, take Willy. Willy was a German prisoner of war who worked for the Mennonite Central Committee in France in 1946. While he was living at our center in France, his wife deserted him for the American soldier by whom she had become pregnant. He had lost all his physical property in Germany; now the only human tie that mattered to him had been callously broken. He was a shattered man. But he found faith through us, and again I was deeply moved by the power of God to work through Christians who seemed inadequate for the task of helping people to faith.

After I returned to the States, I came back to Goshen College and went on to graduate school. I took up again the quest for faith. Again it came largely in connection with revival meetings. I felt the inadequacy of moral goodness, and I felt more keenly the inadequacy of my own faith. Very gradually I began to realize that my quest for faith had been unproductive because I had been looking for the wrong thing. I expected faith to be essentially an emotional experience. I felt I had no faith because God did not come from the outside and bowl me over with a blast of spiritual power. I was made to realize that I was concentrating far too much on myself—on how I should feel about things, and not enough on Christ. Faith, I learned, was not dependent upon my feelings or on anything that I did. It was built on the nature and purpose of

God in His particular acts toward me. I had to let Him work in His own way in His own good time. It would not do to storm the gates of heaven with fervent requests for an emotionalized "spiritual" experience.

God taught me this with no flash of insight. He taught me very gradually, over the course of several years. The media of His teaching, as I look back on them, were probably two, the first of which was Bible study in several courses that I took here. I am one of those who found a much deeper and richer faith at Goshen College. There were two Bible courses especially that helped me: The *Gospel of John,* taught by Howard Charles, and *Romans and Galatians,* taught by Paul Mininger. I found Christ appealing and attractive, more than anyone I had ever encountered before, in the flesh or in my reading. I was not surprised at this discovery, but nevertheless I found the degree of difference striking. And I found Paul wonderfully relevant; before, I had not cared for Paul at all. But Paul spoke to my condition of works-righteousness, particularly in *Romans* and *Galatians;* and he spoke with wisdom and a degree of insight I had not expected.

The second medium was that of counselors—in person and through their writings. J. C. Wenger patiently commiserated with me in my late teens and gave me fatherly advice. Harold S. Bender did the same. Harold Bender also added some sharp comments on some of my improper attitudes; and these comments were highly necessary. God taught me also through the writings of certain persons—Luther more than anyone else, I suppose, because of his experience with works-righteousness and faith. Luther makes delightful reading; he knew how to laugh at himself and to balance the intensity of his own spirit with jests at himself. God taught me through Calvin, through Thomas a Kempis, and Brother Lawrence, and E. Stanley Jones, and C. S. Lewis. I mention these because they are not at all alike. I did not read the works of all of these men in order to get spiritual help, either. I read Luther and Calvin in the course of my academic pursuits in graduate school.

I also read the works of many more men from whom I got no help at all, and this was very discouraging. For example, when I was young, my aunt gave me a book of meditations that my father had liked. It was an inappropriate gift because it was too heavy for me in my tender years. I was mortified to discover that I got nothing at all from the meditations. This was the more distressing because I grew up in an atmosphere which made my father, who died when I was six years old, a saint. Surely I had not a spark of spiritual life in me if these did not move me, I thought! It took me many years to learn the simple truth that human beings who differ in temperament and taste find quite different readings to suit their spiritual needs.

It dawned on me gradually through these experiences that God was speaking through all of these men, not generally but specifically. He was saying: "John, John." I have learned finally what joy is, precisely because I did not pursue it, but because I learned to rely on Christ. In this connection I prize especially John 15:11: "These things I have spoken to you, that my joy may be in you, and that your joy may be full" (RSV). These are well-chosen words. There truly is a fullness of joy in Christ.

24
Completely Changed

RALPH PALMER

I grew up in the city, and I lived in sin. I knew the ropes in the sin game. Among my major sins were drinking, fighting, and gambling. Even today I carry on my body scars of the sinful life which I once lived. Six of my former companions, with whom I used to serve the devil, have met untimely deaths, some in drunken fights, and some at the hands of officers of the law. How I do thank God that my life was spared until I came to the place of repentance! Then the Lord placed a barrier in my way in the form of sickness.

I spent seven weeks in a hospital, but I was returned home more sick than when I left home. Three doctors pronounced my case hopeless, so far as medical science was concerned. They knew of nothing more which they could do for me.

Worst of all, I was still a lost sinner. That I knew very well. I was, indeed, a church member, but I was not a born-again Christian. I was therefore properly terrified, even though the pastor of the church of which I was a member assured me that I had nothing to fear. Was I not a church member? Had I not been a kind and dutiful son? Had I not worked faithfully to help support my fatherless brothers and sisters? After offering a beautiful prayer reminding God that I had belonged to the church for years, and that I had been a good son and brother, he committed me to God's mercy and took his leave.

Ralph Palmer of Newport News, Virginia, has one compelling passion: to know Christ and to make Him known. The evangelistic method to which God has led him is tract distribution, to which he devotes all his time.

Nevertheless, I was in deep despair. I knew I was faced, not with the mercy of God, but with His wrath—and that justly so. My sin rose up like a great mountain before me, and I knew no way to get rid of it.

Suddenly there was a knock at the door, and in walked a Christian woman, a representative of the Warwick River Mennonite Church, at Denbigh, Virginia, a country community about twelve miles from my home. She had been a more or less regular caller at our home in her Christian visitation program. My mother, who had tried in vain to get me to grasp the plan of salvation, then told her of my condition.

"Would you like for me to call my minister to talk to him?" offered the visitor; "I feel sure he can help you."

"Oh, yes, please do so," urged my mother.

An urgent request brought the minister, George R. Brunk, Sr., who was working in his orchard twelve miles away. He came immediately to see the dying man, dropping his work, and soon arriving at my bedside.

How kind he was to me! He quietly and confidently spoke of God's great plan of salvation. He assured me that God would have mercy on me, not because of anything good in me, but because the Lord Jesus Christ had died in order to save me from sin. It was a wonderful story that he told me of a marvelous Saviour. I knew that it must be true, and I accepted it eagerly. I repented of my sin, and put my trust in the Lord Jesus Christ for salvation. I told God that I was in His hands, and if He would spare my life I would serve Him the rest of my days.

In spite of the dire predictions of the doctors I was out of bed the next day, and three days later found me seated in the congregation, the Warwick River Mennonite Church, in the first of a series of evangelistic meetings conducted by R. J. Shenk. Those meetings were a blessing to me, and during that time I made a public confession of my faith in Christ. The neighbors, seeing me time after time seated on my front porch reading my Bible, circulated the report that I was losing my mind! But, thank God, I knew that I had just come to my right mind. My life was completely changed. I was happier than I had ever been, and I began doing what I could to tell others of the Lord Jesus Christ. I also united with the Warwick River Church, and about a year later I was married to a Christian girl, Martha Shenk, a member of the same congregation. On a small lot adjoining the church building we erected our home, living happily there for some years.

I wish that what follows could be omitted from this account. After a few years of Christian living, I began to be a backslider. Little by little I began to nibble at the devil's bait, while a corresponding spiritual coldness toward God crept into my life. My faithful minister saw what was taking place. How well I remember his warning words: "Remember, Ralph, what you promised God when you thought that you were about to die. You told Him if He spared your life, you would serve Him as long as you live. If you turn away from Him now, after all He has done for you, I warn you, He will send upon you something worse than before!"

Later I had occasion to remember well the warning which he gave me. He did not live to see the even more sinful life into which I sank. Neither did he see his prophecy fulfilled in the affliction which God sent upon me, nor my eventual repentance and restoration. But perhaps the angels, who rejoice over a sinner who repents, told him all about it.

For about five years I hardly ever went to church. I fell into worse sins than I had ever been guilty of before. Cigarettes, whiskey, and a pistol were among the things I carried around with me. Unfaithful to God, to the church, and to my family, I was indeed a miserable creature. My wife and little daughter urged me to go with them to church, but I always had an excuse. I think I can truthfully say that I was not really happy for a single minute during that time.

Near the close of this period of backsliding, an incident occurred which made a vivid impression upon me. As a railroad inspector, I had been working at my job all day one Sunday. About 9:30 p.m. a young man from the Warwick congregation came to me. He said only a few words, but they cut me to the heart. He said, "Ralph, I love you, and I want you to be saved," and suddenly he was weeping on my chest. That was too much for me to take. I promised him that I would be in church the next Sunday, and I kept my promise. The memory of that young man's concern was a powerful influence in bringing me back to God.

Then one Sunday morning it struck—the sickness which was again to bring me to death's door, and which the Lord certainly allowed to come upon me, once more to place a barrier across the sinful path that I had been traveling. I had promised my wife to go with her to church on that certain Sunday, but on Saturday evening I backed out, reporting that there was work that I had to do on the railroad the next day. But it was there that the Lord stepped in with His chastening rod. Soon after midnight, early on Sunday morning, I was suddenly stricken with an illness which made it impossible for me to leave my bed. In a few hours, indeed at the very time when I should have been in church, I was delirious. When my brain cleared for a short while, I remembered the warning which my minister had given me years before. I came to hate myself for the life which I had been living, and I began crying to God for forgiveness once more, promising that I would do everything within my power to make restitution for the wrongs which I had done, but God was not yet through with that chastening rod! I became severely ill with rheumatic fever. Months later I emerged from that experience, loathing my former sinful ways, and with a great concern for those who were still held fast in the clutches of the devil as I had been. With special gratitude I must mention the faithful help I received during that sickness from George R. Brunk, Jr., son of my former bishop. It was partly due to his encouragement that I took up the work which has now become my full-time occupation, the distribution of Gospel tracts. I have also received much help and faithful encouragement from my present bishop, Truman H. Brunk, another son of the late George R. Brunk, Sr.

Upon my recovery to good health I was keenly conscious of the thousands of unsaved people who were walking city streets without Christ. I knew exactly how they felt. I had once been one of them. But how could I reach so many people? It looked like a truly impossible task. Certainly, I could not speak personally to each one. Then the thought occurred to me that I could offer them the message of salvation in printed form. My first attempt resulted in the distribution of one thousand tracts in a little over an hour.

Since that small beginning, my tract work has been greatly expanded. I gave up a good-paying railroad job, with thirty years of service, to give my full time to the work of tract distribution. The Lord has wonderfully blessed, and has put it into the hearts of many people to support this tract ministry with their prayers and financial assistance. In fourteen years' time I have given out hand-to-hand on city streets seven and a half million tracts weighing about fifteen tons in cities in forty-eight states and in Canada.

A source of much encouragement to me has been the large number of letters which I have received from people who were helped or led to the Lord through these Gospel messages. Each tract has my imprint, inviting the recipient to write me for further help. We feel that the attractive appearance of high-quality tracts has much to do with their good reception.

I also thank God that there are Christians throughout our congregations who are enough concerned for the salvation of unsaved people that they are willing to give of their means and to support with their prayers this ongoing work. As I engage in the scattering of the precious Seed, the Word of God, I observe that it is still true that some seed falls on hard ground, some on rocky and thorny places, and some on the good soil of honest and good hearts where it grows and brings forth fruit.

The spiritual opposition to this work is sometimes severe. The devil is not pleased; of that I am very sure. I have been threatened by atheists, communists, and other haters of God. Many times I have also been threatened, and even arrested, by policemen who do not like the Gospel message, and who report that they have a city ordinance against tract distribution. But thus far I have never spent a night in jail, nor have I ever paid a fine. An appeal to higher city officials, with a quotation from a recent decision from the United States Supreme Court, upholding the right to distribute such literature, has always brought about my release. We should thank God for a country whose constitution still guarantees freedom of religion, freedom of speech, freedom of the press, and freedom of assembly.

I know of no more effective way to reach the masses of people in our large cities than by the distribution of tracts. I urge the youth of our church to use their time and energy in this great work. May God awaken the church, that we who know the Lord may see the need and hear the call to spread the Gospel far and wide while we still have the opportunity. Ours is the responsibility for the generation in which we live. To the Christian Church comes the command of Christ to bring the Gospel to every creature. We dare not fail to obey.

This account of my work of tract distribution I have given, not to show what I have done, but as a testimony of the great love of Jesus, of His blessings in my life, of His keeping power, and of the means and strength He has given to me to serve Him. All that I have ever done or ever can do is not worth one drop of the precious blood of the Lord Jesus Christ. My whole desire is that my life may be spent in the service of Him who has saved me and done so much for me.

25
I Am a Debtor

ELAINE SOMMERS RICH

If my life has thus far accomplished anything, it is solely through the kindness and grace of God. I can report no blinding flash of light from heaven. It has rather been a constant glow shining more and more, sometimes through periods of personal darkness.

I am a debtor to the home and congregation (Howard-Miami Mennonite, Indiana) in which I grew up. Neither my home nor my congregation was without its problems, yet the supreme value practiced was love.

One incident will illustrate the kind of home we had. I began school in the depression year of 1932 when my father sometimes had to work for a dollar a day. The fifth and last child in our family arrived in November. One first-grade girl came to school barefooted, wearing the same dress day after day. I must have told my mother, for she made the girl a new dress. When I reported this to my teacher, she added a pair of shoes to the outfit. To this day, I remember that girl's face when she appeared in her new clothes.

In our congregation we had people who had completed only six or eight grades of elementary school, and also those who had finished college. Naturally, wide differences of opinion existed, yet I never experienced a "church split"—so damaging to young peo-

Elaine Sommers Rich lives with her husband, Professor Ronald Rich, and their family in North Newton, Kansas. Earlier she taught English in Goshen College. She is a successful writer.

ple—because members of the congregation practiced love and forbearance toward one another. Sunday night and business meetings were open meetings. Anyone, man or woman, could and did speak. It was a thoroughgoing Christian democracy. I am a debtor to my Sunday-school teachers, especially to Eva (Mrs. Chester) Osborne, and to Marjorie (Mrs. Victor) Hochstedler, whose teaching took place in my crucial nine to eleven years.

I was baptized in the spring of 1938 at the age of twelve. For perhaps four years before this I had wished to respond to the evangelistic call, but knew that I was considered much too young. It just was not done. I had to wait. It was not so much a sense of sin that influenced me to join the church as it was a strong love for Christ and a desire to do with my life whatever He wished me to do. On that night, when I publicly responded to the call, my grandfather said to me, "You are just as old as Jesus was when He said, 'Wist ye not that I must be about my Father's business?' "

My home congregation was the school in which, line upon line, precept upon precent, I was brought to a knowledge of Christ and His teaching. To this congregation I remain forever and deeply indebted.

I am a debtor to my public school teachers who opened new worlds of the mind, also God's territory, to me. Earl Whitecotton, debate coach, taught me history, but he also taught me to think. Minnie Alice Parson taught me a keen respect for the English language and for the power of words. To them and others in Greentown school I am a debtor.

In the autumn of 1943 I entered college, where, with the exception of a year in graduate school, I remained for the next ten years, first as a student, then as a teacher. As a college sophomore I survived a period of intense doubt and despair. I was egotistical enough to believe that I could rebut most arguments for Christianity, including St. Augustine's. With my own mind, I sought to erect some kind of logical system which would impose meaning on the universe. One day as I gazed into the race above the Elkhart River, I realized that there was one argument for Christianity which I could not answer. It was the radiant courageous living of Christians whom I knew. How could their lives be explained other than through the power of God? I realized that one must accept God, begin with Him, not reach for Him through premises created by one's own mind.

Goshen College teachers combined intellect and Christian dedication. They showed us that Christianity is relevant in every area of activity and knowledge. They challenged us with the need for Christian pioneering in many areas—peacemaking, missions, economics, mental health, race relations, urban life, youth work. I am deeply indebted to Guy F. Hershberger, John and Roy Umble, Mary Royer, Olive Wyse, Lois Gunden, Carl Kreider, J. C. Wenger, and others. I am a debtor to Goshen College students, both my contemporaries and those whom I later taught. In 1953 I married Ronald Rich. His concept of the greatness of God is based on his knowledge of the physical universe, of atoms and galaxies. I am a debtor to him, to his family, and to our four children. I am a debtor to the General Conference Mennonites of Kansas among whom I have lived for the past years.

This list of people to whom I am indebted is quite incomplete. I should mention authors of books, Friends' meetings, two professors at Michigan State University, the Mennonite Central Committee, the Mennonite Publishing House, relatives, neighbors in North Newton, Kansas, and so on and on.

The love that is in Christ has most often been revealed to me through the loving ministry of other people. May His kingdom come, His will be done, on earth as it is in heaven!

26
Taking God into Business

AL RICHARDS

On January 4, 1918, I was born in a small remodeled log cabin in De Kalb County, Indiana, the first of seven children. My father had been left to shift for himself from an early age. His father had died when my father was only six months old. His mother died when I was in my early teens. The only information which I can find about this side of the family is that they were from the East. They had traveled as far West as Nebraska to homestead. Their first home was a sod hut. In time the droughts and sandstorms drove them back East. When they got as far as Indiana, they stopped and settled near Auburn. My father, with very little schooling, went to work, living where he could until he met my mother. He then established a home of his own. My mother's side of the family is just as obscure, since my grandmother was an orphan. I never learned of what nationality my grandfather was. I do remember my grandmother as a very godly person, and my grandfather as one who always made fun of the church. This was probably my only contact with Christianity in my early years.

My parents truly loved us as children. I remember the excitement and joy that was theirs when they were able to buy new clothes for all the family. One time they bought us a pony, wagon, and harness that must have been a great sacrifice for them. I know that they did not have enough money to meet their ever-present expens-

---

Al Richards has a number of factories which drill diamond dies for the manufacture of wire. He is an active member of the First Mennonite Church of Fort Wayne, Indiana.

es, but they tried to get us everything we needed. Consequently, my childhood was a very happy one.

Christianity was not known in our home. I suppose we were probably invited to church at one time or another. I do remember that we went to church when I was about ten or twelve. My mother played the piano at church, but at the same time my parents were in charge of the dances two or three times a week. At these dances my mother played, my father "called," and I learned most of the steps before I reached my teens. Later, when I was almost sixteen we lost through the Depression everything that we as a family had worked for. After the sheriff's sale, my father was left with seven children and no means to provide for them. When I wanted to go to school activities, or have a date, my mother would gather the eggs, and give them to me to sell at the grocery so that I would have the money to go.

As I grew older, and graduated from high school, I felt that I was a burden at home, and so I went to Fort Wayne to live and work. I had neither a job nor a room, but eventually found one after days of walking. My first job was working in a tavern for five dollars a week, including tips, which did not amount to much. The hours were long, and I became somewhat bitter, thinking that if I ever got the opportunity, I would get two jobs working days and nights, Saturdays and Sundays, until I was able to get the things I wanted. Eventually I did get a better job, unloading steel and coal, and even worked my way into the shop. I also got another and "better" job, that of tending bar and waiting tables at a night club.

In the meantime, my parents had moved into the neighborhood of the Anderson Mennonite Church. This is the first time that I had ever heard the word "Mennonite." To me it was just another cult. When I heard what their beliefs were, and that my folks were joining that church, I did not like it any better. Of course, I knew that everyone should be free to do what he wanted to, and out of respect for my parents I went to visit the church. I had decided to live at home and drive into town to work, but when they told me that our home would be different since they had joined the church, I decided to move again to an apartment in town.

The next few years I choose to leave blank. They are under the blood of our Lord Jesus Christ.

I married a good wife of German Lutheran background. We became the parents of two children, Steve and Jerry. Both my wife and I worked. I had an opportunity to get in on the ground floor of a new business. Since the pay was nil, it was work at two jobs with my wife continuing to work, so that I could keep my interest in the business. The business prospered. I became the traveling representative and covered the United States and Canada. In my work I followed the pattern, "Wine and dine," to get new business and to keep the old. It never occurred to me that there could be another way. There was a certain emptiness, however, in gaining an account this way. I suspect now that my sense of emptiness might have resulted from the prayers of my parents following me wherever I went.

The people from the Mennonite Church continued to come to visit us. They were "nice," but I didn't want any part of their religion! We decided to go to another church. This was to satisfy the hunger that had begun to well up in our souls. This other church would have permitted us to continue living the way we wished to. This lasted for about a year, but only brought us more dissatisfaction. Finally, one day Preacher J. S. Neuhouser, from the Anderson Mennonite Church, stopped in and again asked us to give our lives to Christ. We yielded. This was the day we met God! And we determined to live our lives for Him. Amos Zehr and many others were a help to us in the following weeks.

After we had made our decision to follow Christ, it dawned upon me what this would mean as far as business was concerned. In fact, to me it meant that I would have to give it up. I knew that the way in which we had operated would conflict with my new standards and convictions. Yet, there was a struggle within me when I remembered the effort which was involved in building the business, and the sacrifices our family had made to get a little security. I walked into the office the next day and told my partners of my decision. I stated that I would sell my interest in the business, but they asked me to stay and try it for a while.

To prove my sincerity I made a trip through the East, telling all the customers of my decision. I had thought that they would laugh at me, or maybe write to the office about my strange actions. Much to my surprise, most of them congratulated me, and said that they wished that they had the strength to do the same. This added much fuel to my zeal!

I have learned to rely on God for my strength. Many times I have had to take inventory and rededicate my life. I have also found many Christian businessmen, and I know that God is using them as surely as He uses a missionary in the darkest continent.

If my past activities were to be reviewed before God and myself, even I could pronounce my fatal doom. I am indeed grateful for the Lord Jesus Christ who alone is able to bridge this needy gap. My earlier life was not a good testimony; it was rather a miscarriage in the plan of God.

It is my desire that if our sons are called upon to give their testimony, it may be filled with the closeness of God in our home.

27
God Creates a Pastor

STANLEY D. SHANTZ

I was born in a prairie farm home to Addison C. and Priscilla Devitt Shantz, in the new district of Guernsey, Saskatchewan, on May 23, 1914, the oldest in a family of three sons. It was the first year of World War I, and this war baby was destined to face the same decisions which many other World War I babies had to face, when World War II came. My father and mother had their family background close to Kitchener, Ontario. Father, along with many other young men, had visions of establishing a home of his own in Western Canada. At the turn of the century he began working for Jacob Bergey near Rosser, Manitoba. After four years of steady work, and equipped with six hundred dollars, he moved to Saskatchewan, where he and his brother Jonathan homesteaded between Watrous and Guernsey, after an arduous trip of 120 miles with four oxen which they had purchased in Regina, the capital of Saskatchewan. This continued as a brother relationship until my father returned to Ontario in 1912 to marry the woman who had waited for him. They had grown up on neighboring farms and both had attended the Mannheim school. My uncle continued to make his home with my parents until his death in 1939.

Father and Mother never placed their membership in the Mennonite Church which is located near Guernsey, Saskatchewan.

Stanley D. Shantz is a Christian minister in Edmonton, Alberta; a member of the Executive Committee of the Alberta-Saskatchewan Mennonite Conference, and a youth leader.

As a young man my father had united with the Mennonite Church in Ontario, but it remained for the Methodist Church in Manitoba to clarify for him the new birth experience. After counseling with his parents in Ontario by letter, he decided to affiliate with the Methodist Church. He never changed this affiliation, even when the Methodist Church which he was attending in Saskatchewan officially amalgamated with the new United Church of Canada. My mother was a member of the "New Mennonites" (United Missionary Church now) in Ontario, and never altered her membership, even when she married. I describe this situation, not because it was ideal, but because in spite of it my parents' attitude was such that it inspired my two brothers and me to remain by our first choice of a church home after committing our lives to Christ. The attitude of our parents had much to do with this. Never once did we hear them argue over matters of religion, and they were always careful not to needlessly criticize ministers of any church in the presence of their children.

In our parental home we learned to appreciate the sweat of hard and honest work. The experiences of the Depression of the 1930's left a deep impression on us as we learned to value and save hard-earned money.

Our parents saw to it that their boys had the privilege of regular attendance at the Mennonite Church in their community, even though my father spent many a Sunday afternoon at the United Church, which met in a neighboring schoolhouse, either teaching a class or acting as Sunday-school superintendent. At this point our parents must have sensed that their boys would need the association and teaching which is found in the Mennonite Church if they were to blossom spiritually. Here it was that periodic revival meetings were held, and where ultimate association with Christian young people would be a possibility.

It was at the age of twelve years that I first sensed clearly my need of a Saviour. I still vividly remember sitting on the back bench of the church building, under deep conviction of sin—not any special sin, but a deep-rooted sense of a need for Christ. I refused the Spirit's call even when many others of my friends responded. My interest in spiritual things remained keen during the next two years. I would read my Bible occasionally, and never neglected to continue some form of prayer life. My interest in the teaching of the Second Coming of Christ was keen, and whenever a minister spoke on this subject I sat riveted to the bench with interest. I recall how during the summer evenings before retiring I would sit at my bedroom window watching the sky and wondering if Jesus would come that night. In my boyhood thinking I had planned to quickly accept Jesus as my Saviour should I see signs of His appearance in the sky. At this point some good Bible teaching on forgiveness for children would have been a tremendous help.

At the age of fourteen, when John Grove served as evangelist, I finally accepted Christ as my Saviour. I recall with clarity the last Sunday afternoon of the meetings when the evangelist came to our home and spoke privately to several of the young people who had gathered in our house for the afternoon. Very vividly do I remember repeating in his presence, "God be merciful to me a sinner." The experience of forgiveness was real. I knew that Jesus was my Saviour. That evening I went forward during the first verse of the invitation hymn to confess my Saviour before men. I recall with joy the warm handshake extended to me by the bishop of the church, Eli S. Hallman, and the kiss with which my father greeted me at the close of the service. Also I recall the elation that seemed to flood me even physically as I ran, so it seemed, on wings from the car shed to the house later that evening. Beside the stove in the kitchen stood my father, rolling up his tie, and as I came in he spoke to me, "Do you know what you did tonight, Stan?"

"Yes," I replied. "I accepted Christ as my Saviour."

"Never turn your back on God," was my father's response.

This simple admonition, more than any other statement my father ever made to me, helped to steady and hold me to my commitment to Christ during the tempestuous years of adolescence and young manhood. At the time of my conversion, Mother was visiting in Ontario, and my brother and I deeply appreciated the letter of encouragement we received from her when Father wrote and said that the two of us had made decisions for Christ.

A decision concerning baptism and a church home now needed to be made. One morning in the bedroom while Mother was straightening up the room and making the bed, she took the opportunity of talking to my brother Arnold and me about it. She made it clear that it would be their wish as parents that we would become members of the Mennonite Church. We then talked to the bishop, M. H. Schmitt, who had succeeded Bishop Hallman during the summer, about it, and his warm assurance that we would be welcomed helped us decide in that direction. As was customary in those years, instruction for baptism was given openly, preceding the morning message, while those for whom it was given sat on the front bench. I was baptized with a number of other young people in September, 1928. We missed not having our parents present to enjoy the Lord's Supper with us in those early years. Had it not been for several suggestions and attitudes expressed by my parents at timely points, I think I might have lost interest in the Christian life and the church of my choice.

I recall with clarity a certain Sunday when communion was to be observed. Family plans had previously been made for our entire family to visit my mother's brother and family, and to keep this appointment necessitated missing the communion service. As we drove past the corner where we would have turned to the church, I can still hear Father saying to us over his shoulder as he was driving, "Next Sunday, boys, we will tell Mr. Schmitt where you were today, so he will not begin to wonder why you were not present." This was done. Brother Schmitt deeply appreciated this explanation, and as a pastor in later years I would also many a time have appreciated such clarifying explanations. I think this incident did much to stabilize our relationship with the Mennonite Church.

My early experiences of salvation were never disqualified in my thinking, even though there were incidents of sin that touched my life and brought me afresh to Christ seeking forgiveness. I remember vividly the night when in a special service I dedicated my life to Christ. For several years I had been busy as a Sunday-school teacher, leading in singing, participating in young people's work, and literary society meetings. The decision for further training and preparation for service was made when T. K. Hershey, one of our church's first missionaries to Argentina, held meetings at the Sharon Church.

My first step in preparation for Christian service was to complete high school. I had already finished three years by correspondence courses from the Saskatchewan curriculum, and for the fourth year I found it necessary to leave home and board in a neighboring town. This was during the 1930's sometimes called "the hungry 30's" when very few young people completed high school. All I allowed myself in spending money over and above board, room, and tuition, was ten cents a week for chocolate bars. This was a discipline I still cherish.

With high school completed I went to Ontario in the fall of 1937 and worked three months for $5.00 a week at a cousin's place, doing general farm work, which included following a walking plow, pulled by a twenty-four-year-old team in a field of clay soil embedded with alfalfa roots as thick as your thumb!

When the Ontario Mennonite Bible School opened the following winter, I was glad for the opportunity to sit under the teaching of such men of God as S. F. Coffman, Oscar Burkholder, C. F. Derstine, and J. B. Martin. Their Scriptural and consistent teaching left a vital impression on my life. We enjoyed the Bible school but returned home in the spring to help Father on the farm. It seemed that the way did not open for me to complete the three-year course at Ontario Mennonite Bible School. Consequently I enrolled for a five-month winter term in an interdenominational Bible school at Regina, Saskatchewan. I recall many of the experiences in this with pleasure, even though there were definite weaknesses in their teaching. Emphasis was placed on personal witnessing, Bible memory work, and concentrated study, along with the discussions of dormitory life which helped to strengthen my desire to be of service for Christ. By the second year this Bible school had been taken over by the Evangelical Church, and I was given an invitation to accept membership in that denomination, as I would have the opportunity of eventually becoming a minister in their fellowship. But there was one barrier I could not hurdle. This denomination did not teach nonresistance as accepted and taught so faithfully in the Mennonite churches in Alberta by C. J.

Ramer, M. D. Stutzman, Ezra Stauffer, and others, during short Bible schools held in the winter months. Some of these short-term schools I had attended, and the clear teaching on nonresistance gave me a positive conviction in this area. The invitation to accept membership in a church that refused this teaching consequently had to be turned aside.

The next few years had their periods of frustration, indecision, and at times resentment. Always I had wanted to take more schooling, but when upon completion of high school I wanted to attend a university, there was no money for such a venture. I introduced my father to the principal of the high school in a vain attempt to convince him that I should go to the university. This may have been a blessing in disguise, as the war years would have found me in an institution that placed much emphasis on military training. World War II also prevented my attending one of our church schools in the United States. This I have often regretted. However, the past cannot be undone, and I realize that I can only do my best for God's glory, using the training and ability at my disposal.

It was in the middle twenties of my life that I learned to know and appreciate and eventually love the one whom God had intended for me as my life companion. She was the only one with whom I shared my conviction for the ministry. She had a steadying influence on my life. In June of 1943, at the age of twenty-nine, I was ordained to the ministry for the Sharon Church near Guernsey, Saskatchewan, by J. B. Stauffer and C. J. Ramer. Almost two years later I was united in marriage to Fern Burkhart, who also had been active in our local church. In the ensuing years, through experiences that have been both bitter and sweet, her consistent life and spiritual support have enriched my ministry. During the annual conference of July, 1952, I was ordained to the office of bishop.

Like others, our experiences have been varied. Some we recall with pleasure, and others would perhaps better be forgotten. Altogether we have spent sixteen years on our farm, in which time God has given us four precious children. We have deeply appreciated the environment of farm life for our children, but must admit that the demands of the farm robbed me of time to study, visit, and do my church work. I have always had a conviction that this arrangement was unscriptural.

Many ministers face a crisis at some period in their ministry. I was no exception. It is a difficult thing to experience misunderstanding that is caused by personal mannerisms and the way the truth is presented. However, it was a refining process for me to view circumstances objectively, taking counsel with my companion as to the cause for certain situations, and to maintain an attitude of love toward all the brothers and sisters in the Lord, as we searched our own hearts and tried to stand by personal convictions. Such experiences in developing Christian maturity were most valuable when we learned not to needlessly react to people, but to allow time, consistency, and God's hand to overrule in these experiences. Today we are grateful for them.

More recent experiences in the Lord's work have been ours when in the winters of 1960 and 1961 it was our privilege as an entire family to spend a total of seven months in the Calling Lake area of Alberta, helping temporarily as pastor in a mission church environment. This has been helpful in better understanding circumstances which missionaries face when they thrust out into the frontiers of mission work, and seek to establish a group fellowship that is Christian. This was a valuable experience in helping to give us guidance in recent years in the work of the Alberta-Saskatchewan Mission Board as its president.

I wish that as a child and in my early teens there would have been clearer teaching on the privilege of enjoying forgiveness, even prior to the conversion experience. The sense of forgiveness is also for us to enjoy with and after conversion. Simply stated, the new birth experience is ours by faith so that we can gain victory over the *practice* of sin, in order that the necessity of seeking forgiveness for moral failure will become increasingly less as we grow in grace and in the knowledge of Christ. One experience in restitution which I faced after being ordained as a minister still comes clearly to my memory. As a school boy I had stolen a few cents from my brother's "piggy bank" to make partial payment on a prize tool I bought from the man who often stopped at our school. The man moved away and I still owed him seventeen cents. Occasionally the Holy Spirit would remind me of this unsettled boyhood episode. Finally, years later, I addressed a letter to this man, who now lived in the Peace River area of Alberta, and enclosed enough money to provide for the interest and principal of this old debt.

World War II also brought an experience that stands out sharply in my recollection as an evidence of God's guidance. I was called upon to face Judge Embury and to establish my claim for recognition as a conscientious objector to war. I spent considerable time looking up Scripture verses and Biblical answers to support my convictions. The judge asked me a key question, and the Holy Spirit instantly brought to my mind a most satisfactory answer that was drawn from my previous knowledge of the Bible and my experience with Christ. The judge accepted the answer without question. This experience taught me that God honors constant preparation from His Word and a continuous relation with Christ.

In my work I want to sense the frustration which many young people face today in their desire to serve their Lord and find an acceptable and useful place of service. The convictions which others expressed to me at various points in my life and my youth helped to impel me toward the preparation I made for service. Possibly my faith was not strong enough to overcome the obstacles that blocked the path for the schooling I longed to have. However, we dare not bemoan the thought of "being born twenty years too soon." I must go on, facing the situations as I find them, and trying with God's help to serve the generation in which I find myself.

> I will not ask to know the future years,
> Nor cloud today with dark tomorrow's fears;
> I only ask a light from heaven to show
> How, step by step, my pilgrimage will go.

28
Lifelong Learning from Christ

ELAM W. STAUFFER

I was born on January 20, 1899, and raised on a farm on the banks of the big Chiquies Creek, four miles south of Manheim, Pennsylvania. I was third in a family of five. The youngest, the only sister we had, died at the age of eight years. My parents, Benjamin R. and Fanny Weidman Stauffer, were hardworking people, making an honest living, endeavoring to raise their children for God. We enjoyed good health, hard work, and good food and care. Living on the farm brought us a sense of security from the usual restless world. All church services were attended, and all activities participated in as far as possible. When Sunday school was first started at our church, it was held in the afternoon. When our parents could not take us, we walked the two miles, often barefooted, in order to attend.

My memories of home are of early rising to help do the barn chores before breakfast, of working in the fields, of swimming and fishing in the creek in summer, and of trapping and skating in the winter. Books were not numerous in our home. I especially remember the Bible, a Bible story book, *Pilgrim's Progress,* and Theodore Roosevelt's accounts of his visit to Africa to hunt big game. Early Bible reading was from a sense of duty rather than an attempt to get to know and have fellowship with God. I did have the consciousness of sin and my lost condition early in life,

---

Elam W. Stauffer is a Christian minister from Lancaster County, Pennsylvania, who has labored for several decades in Africa, and as bishop of the Tanganyika Mennonite Church.

but because I was unwilling to yield, I was beset by many a fear of dying unsaved and by dreams of the world coming to an end.

I attended a small public school, one and one-half miles from my home, until I was seventeen years old. Then after persistent requests my parents permitted me to enter Millersville State Normal school for the spring term of 1916. Here I studied for two and a half years, preparing to teach school. At this time I realized that the longer I put off becoming a Christian, and the farther I went on in school, the harder it would be to begin. During the fall months of 1916 I stood to accept Christ as my Saviour at evangelistic meetings being held by I. B. Good at the Landisville Church. I was conscious that I was a sinner, and that I could escape eternal judgment only by accepting Christ. I was sincere in the step I took, although I sought salvation mainly as an "insurance policy" against eternal damnation. I received no catechetical instruction, nor did anyone fully explain the plan of salvation to me, nor do I remember anyone counseling or praying with me in this period of my life. I was baptized at Erisman's, my home church, by Bishop Isaac B. Brubaker.

The problem in my new life was that, though I tried to conduct myself as a Christian, I did not want to get too far removed from my unsaved friends. I received encouragement from my parents and Christian friends, but few of these felt able to say that they knew that they were saved. This was even considered presumptuous by many. Warnings against sin and worldliness were plentiful, but little was said of entering into the fullness of life in Christ. This gave me an unsatisfactory Christian experience. No assurance of present salvation, no testimony for Christ, and no real joy in my Christian life! When I heard some people say that a person should know that he is saved, I became concerned about my state and decided that this matter was too important to neglect. Having heard from others how a person could know that he is saved, I took my Bible, knelt by my bedside, and confessed my sins. Then placing my finger on John 3:16; 3:36; 5:24; and I John 5:12, I put my faith in Christ and gave my life to Him. I arose with joy and assurance in my heart. I had taken God at His word, and He absolutely cannot lie.

As a young Christian I lived a good moral life, was accepted of men, and was used in the church in Sunday-school work. This gave me a sense of righteousness, but little understanding of grace, or of the liberty of the Spirit, or of the deep spiritual need in my own heart. For me salvation consisted of keeping from sinful acts, and of living according to the right standards of my society. I did not recognize as sins judging others, bitterness, impure thoughts, pride in its various forms, and the many other subtle sins which men so easily overlook. I had more concern about what I did than what I really was before God. I had a zeal for the work of the church, rather than for God to work His will in and through me.

In my early teens I had a consciousness that God would someday call me to some specific task for Him. I have often regretted that I did nothing to prepare for that call. While studying at Millersville, and later while teaching public school, I came in closer contact with Christians of other denominations. This larger fellowship brought to me a hunger to know more of God and of the fellowship of His people. After marrying Elizabeth Kauffman I began to farm. During this time, we began to help in rural mission work at Cornwall. I also shared in the lot with others for possible ordination at Erisman's. Martin Metzler was chosen as pastor. I fear my main burden during this time was to lead men to my kind of Christianity, rather than to a deep knowledge of God and of the fullness of life and surrender to Him. I praise God for His long patience with me and for using me as He could. Service in the church brought a certain joy, but also a complacency and false security, for it blinded me to my deepest soul need.

In 1933 my wife and I were asked by our church to go to East Africa to open foreign work under the Eastern Board. After prayer, we believed it was God's call for us and accepted. O. O. Miller and I left New York on December 7, 1933, to visit various offices along the way to Africa and to seek a field. This was an entirely new experience to me. I could only go along, listen, and seek to learn. God led us to Tanganyika. The Mosemanns and my wife followed. Early in April, 1934, the five of us met in Dar es Salaam to plan for the opening of work in Tanganyika.

Being removed from our home culture and working beside

others of God's servants, with different designations and emphases, soon produced a testing of reality in my own soul. Did I really believe what I taught? Were these really eternal truths? Would my message work in a heathen culture? Was I teaching what I did not possess myself? Were the things I emphasized the ones that God holds important? These and many other questions pressed for an answer. A sense of great inadequacy, and a longing for a more intimate knowledge of God came upon me. Studying, praying, working, and searching increased the longing. After eight years of service, I realized that I was not communicating Jesus Christ to these people. Then I, with others, cried to God to come down on us to meet our own need. God in His own ways revealed Calvary as the place where God came down to deal with sin, self, and all that opposes Him. At Calvary God meets men's need and communicates Himself to them. Here is the only place for a man in need.

To take the place of a needy soul is not easy for a person accepted by men and of long service in the church, but I was desperately hungry, and knew that only here could I meet God. What sinfulness of heart God showed me as I stood in His holy presence! I had to learn that after years of Christian living and service there was still absolutely nothing good in me. All the goodness and righteousness I could muster were just filthy rags before Him in whose presence I now stood. I began to see myself somewhat as in Job 42:5. Not what I do but what I really am before God became my concern.

During my Christian life, God had brought several deeply spiritual men into close relationship with me. These men, too, had made me hunger for what they had, and what I did not have. These men stand out clearly in my memory. Now God again brought brothers and sisters of the foreign land into our midst to show me what living with Jesus meant. These did not pose as righteous before men, nor did they try to hide from God their true selves. They confessed openly and acknowledged themselves to be sinners, in need of grace. They constantly looked to Jesus for cleansing and filling, and He was doing it. They were full of praises for Him, and His sufficiency for them. How He satisfies when all other hope is gone! This is all of grace. Who can claim any "faithfulness" here? Who need justify failures when simple repentance cleanses the soul? Who may dare to claim any credit? Grace is for poor needy souls who have no other claim before God. At heart all men are alike. The "good" and "righteous" are as lost as the vilest sinner. I could now agree with the speaker who had told us, "If you will look at the vilest wretch in the gutter, and thank God that you are not as bad as he, you have sin in your heart." It was a Pharisee who prayed with himself, "God, I thank thee, that I am not as other men are." I came to understand John Knox, who, seeing the murderer being led out to his execution, said, "But for the grace of God, there goes John Knox."

Walking thus with God permitted Him to enter into all of life. Our home became new; the work became His; I had a new relationship to those among whom I lived and served. I could not hope to give them anything in myself, for I was utterly undone, even as they, but I could point them to Him who was meeting my need for forgiveness, love, faith, joy, peace, strength, and every other need. On our first furlough, 1938-39, we learned that my wife had a weak heart. We were warned that she might pass away quickly any time. For eight years we lived together with a consciousness that we might suddenly be parted. This served as a sanctifier for both of us. We walked together with God as far as I could go with her until on June 17, 1947, while I was by her bedside in the Mengo Hospital at Kampala, radiant with joy she passed on into glory.

I was still in the flesh. Again I knelt by my bedside and committed myself unto God in my new situation for His keeping and glory. He gave me Jude 24 as an anchor. For two years God graciously sustained and satisfied me in new trials, temptations, and relationships. I could now testify to new proofs of His sufficiency, living as a widower. My brethren and sisters in Christ, in challenges and fellowship, were used of God to help me accept myself as I am, and to go to God constantly for forgiveness, cleansing, and fullness.

After two years, God joined me to Grace Metzler in a new bond in Christ. We were married on June 3, 1949. The blending of two lives into one is never an easy process, but together walking with Jesus means enjoying His wonderful grace in every situation.

This marriage exposed new needs in my soul. My theories of rearing children did not prove perfect, patience was short, wisdom insufficient, and the flesh ever ready to rise to take over. How I praise God that Grace and I had learned to walk with God, by admitting our deep needs, challenging each other to His highest, and looking to the precious blood to cleanse us daily. More than ever we leaned on our constant Companion for what we needed for life.

As the church grew, the burden of bishop responsibility grew too. Ordinations came on. How were these to be conducted? The African leaders needed teaching, training, and guidance in areas in which I had no training. Integration of mission and church came in 1960. Every task and change demanded abilities that I did not have. How human wisdom and the flesh tried to take over! But also how faithfully God, through the challenges of my brethren and sisters, constantly revealed to me my own need, and took me to Christ, the never-failing supply of whatever I needed at the time. The farther I went on with God, the more sinful and undone I saw myself to be, the more forgiving, gracious, and utterly satisfying He proved Himself to be.

Yes, I met God early in life and found myself to be a sinner. I sought salvation in Christ. Through the years I met Him in times and ways of His own planning. It is perhaps better to say that through the years God has graciously and steadfastly followed me to draw me to Himself. Each time He revealed Himself anew to me, I saw more of myself as I really am. When I see this, I cease to have any hope except for His provision for me in Jesus Christ. When pressure of work, or of circumstances, or of sin in some subtle form dims the sense of His holy presence, then I realize again that I am launching out on my own, and that self is ruling. Then I need to bow at the foot of the cross anew, and drawing near to God ask His forgiveness and cleansing in the precious blood of the Lamb, and rejoice anew at the marvels of His grace. I shall thus go on with Him until I meet Him face to face in glory with the blood-washed throng. Then I shall praise Him as I ought.

29
A Communist Converted

ERNESTO SUAREZ

On April 28, 1920, I was born in Buenos Aires, the capital city of Argentina. My parents were Spaniards and of course Roman Catholic. Three different times we removed from Argentina to Spain, the last time when I was eleven years of age. We children attended the Catholic Church, and my two brothers and I were baptized as infants and later confirmed in that church. When I was a high-school student (in Spain the high-school course lasts five years and the pupils are from thirteen to seventeen years of age), both the Communist and Socialist parties had strong influence among the students. What seemed to me as the fanatical and obscurantist attitude of the Roman Catholic Church became intolerable. This was also the experience of many other students.

My oldest brother, an active socialist, one time gave me a Spanish book with the title, *Religion for the Common People,* by J. N. Ibarreta. This book abounded with quotations from the Bible, and the author rejected every Biblical point of view on "scientific grounds." He opposed the Genesis account of the creation particularly. At first I could not believe the assertions of the book. For myself I had never read the Bible, as is the case with many Latin-American Catholics. I began to wonder if the Bible did contain such blunders as Ibarreta asserted. Therefore I purchased a Bible—the first one I had had in my life—in order to

---

Ernesto Suárez is a Mennonite minister living in Argentina. He edits the evangelical periodical, *El Discípulo Cristiano,* which serves the Spanish world.

check whether the quotations were genuine. To my astonishment I found that the author had quoted the verses which he chose verbatim. Of course, he had chosen the passages which suited his purpose, taking them out of context. In this way it became easy to reject almost everything. But this erroneous approach was not apparent to me at that point. What did impress me was the author's position that if the Bible was truly the Word of God, then modern science demonstrates that God knew nothing about the physical world! That is, there really is no God. These arguments, along with my earlier antipathy to Roman Catholicism, led me to become a complete, yet sincere atheist.

From this point in my life I devoted my energies to attempting to make converts from Catholicism to atheism. I began at home, trying to convince my parents and my younger brothers, then my friends and fellow students. My program of "evangelism" for atheism resembled the great commission given by Jesus Christ to His disciples!

Actually I found the step from atheism to communism to be a short one. Some older men of the Communist party took advantage of our naive atheistic convictions. Their agent was generally a clever and popular student with leadership abilities. Such a gifted communist found it easy to win me and others to his point of view, and so, little by little, I was led into the camp of the communists. I became a fanatical admirer of the Soviet Union.

When the Spanish Civil War broke out in 1936, only a serious disease prevented me from leaving home and joining the Republican army, which in my province of Asturias was largely composed of socialist and communist volunteers. For two and a half years we endured all sorts of privation and difficulties, during which time my atheism was of no help to me at all. I very much desired to return to Argentina, but this was impossible because of Franco's blockade. When at last Franco's troops occupied the city in which I was living, I began to look forward to my repatriation. Meanwhile a law was passed by which all children of resident Spaniards were considered as Spanish, regardless of place of birth.

At eighteen years of age I was drafted into Franco's army, and sent to another city for military training. This was during the decisive days of the Spanish Civil War. In the barracks I became ill and was sent home for a thirty-day period of convalescence.

At this point a very unusual incident occurred. I had been looking for permission to leave Spain as an Argentine citizen, but the military law had declared me to be a Spanish citizen. And now that I was drafted into the army I had found it impossible to leave Spain. To my amazement a few days before my thirty-day convalescent leave expired, I received a thick envelope from the Spanish Secretary of the Interior granting me a safe-conduct to leave Spain.

This was incredible! At first both my father and I considered it a trick to catch me at the frontier, but finally we decided that I should take the risk. My father accompanied me as far as the Spanish-Portuguese frontier. At that point I was permitted to cross into Portugal without incident.

At that time there were about seven thousand Latin Americans, born of Spanish parents, who were living in Spain. All of them between eighteen and thirty-five years of age were drafted into Franco's army. It may be that I was the only one who was able to escape. Human reasoning would say that my release was due to the confusion of those war times. I now know, however, that the real reason was God's love for me, poor sinner that I was. I was back in Argentina, and was again employed at my occupation of printer.

But in spite of my good health, I was not a happy man. I was still a communist and an atheist, but I no longer had an enthusiasm for this position. Rather, I felt angry at everybody and everything. I hated British imperialism, feeling that it was British companies which dominated Argentina's economy. I also hated Yankee imperialism, feeling that North America possessed an economic monopoly in the Latin-American countries. Consequently when the second World War broke out, my sympathies were with Germany. This was not at all because of Hitler. It was rather because, as many other Latin Americans felt, only a British defeat at the hands of the Germans would give to us the opportunity to get out from under England's heavy control over Argentina's economy. Our philosophy was something like this: "Let the Germans defeat the British, and we will keep ourselves neutral."

Little by little I became an Argentine nationalist. This may seem to be a surprising change of mind, but the disappointments of life and my own state of unbelief undoubtedly played a major role in this change.

And now we come to the revelation of God's love. In 1942, when I was twenty-two years of age, I was living in a rented room in a boarding house. My roommate was a Christian young man, also twenty-two years of age, whose manner and speech fascinated me from the beginning. He was different from all the people that I had ever known. One Friday evening he said to me: "I would like to invite you to a meeting of evangelical young people tomorrow evening."

When I heard the word "evangelical," I remembered that Bible in Spain, and how I had lost respect for all religion. I laughed to myself and thought: "Poor fellow, he is a good boy! No doubt about that. But he still believes in the Bible. He does not know that modern science has demonstrated that there is no God." But my respect for the young man was so great that I felt constrained to accept his invitation. Consequently I went to the meeting.

At the evangelical Christian meeting I met a large number of other "peculiar" young people. They made a deep impression on me. I found them very friendly, utterly sincere! Such people I had never known existed, either as Catholics, atheists, communists, or nationalists! Prior to coming to the meeting I had asked my roommate who the minister was. He replied that he was an American. (His name was L. S. Weber, a Canadian Mennonite missionary.) I was so strongly prejudiced against all North Americans that this created an additional difficulty for me. At that time I felt that the Argentine press was dominated by the Allies, and with the exception of one or two newspapers, the headlines and articles were negative toward the Germans and the Japanese. Since this pastor was a North American, I *knew* that he would hate his enemies to the utmost. But it was not so! At first I suspected some hypocrisy on his part, and so I began asking him tricky questions about the Germans. This continued for some time. To my astonishment I discovered that he actually loved the Germans. Of course, he was not in favor of what they were doing, and he was ready to admit freely the many sins on the part of the Allies. This, in spite of being an "American"!

This really moved me. Imagine finding a man who even in time of war was able to love his enemy. To me this seemed unbelievable. I had had much experience of people hating one another. The communist hated the capitalist, the workers hated the employers, the nationalists hated the imperialists, and so forth.

Little by little I began to admit to myself that this must be a good religion. These people are not Catholic, but Protestant. And they talk so much about the Bible! So once again I began to read the Bible. Even though many things were at first not clear to me, the ringing testimony of these good people encouraged me to continue with my reading. In March, 1943, I attended a Young People's Retreat which was organized by the Mennonites. My prejudices by this time had become much weaker.

During the last night of the retreat I had a deep spiritual experience. I clearly saw myself as I really was, a lost sinner. I confessed my sins and wept and the next day I gave my public testimony before over a hundred young people. I had been born again!

One year after my conversion I heard the call to become a minister of Jesus Christ. Consequently I enrolled in our Bible Institute and spent four years in study there. Upon my graduation in 1947 I was appointed pastor of the Tres Lomas Mennonite congregation. Meanwhile, in 1946 I had married a young woman who was also a student in the Bible Institute. In 1950 I was ordained to the Mennonite ministry. For seven years I served as editor of the official organ of the Mennonite Church in Argentina, *La Voz Menonita* (The Mennonite Voice). In 1955 I received a scholarship which enabled me to study for one year, 1955-56, at Goshen College Biblical Seminary. Upon my return to Argentina I was appointed pastor of the Trenque Lauquen congregation. For four years I was also in charge of the *Luz y Verdad* (Spanish Mennonite Broadcast, *Light and Truth*) office for South America. In 1962 I was appointed as pastor of the Salto congregation. But increasingly I had been devoting my energies to Christian literature. I served, for example, as editor-in-chief of the Spanish Mennonite magazine, *El Discipulo Cristiano* (*The Christian Disciple*) with circulation in all of Latin America, Spain, and the United States. In 1962 it was also my privilege to spend two and a half months attending the first International Christian Writers' Seminar at Green Lake, Wisconsin. This was a most helpful experience. Part of my time was also devoted to the task of translating books into Spanish for Christian nursery pupils.

Thus my spiritual pilgrimage has been long and painful: from Roman Catholicism to atheism—to communism—to nationalism—and finally to a vital Christianity. My final word is that of the New Testament: "There is salvation in no one else, for there is no other name under heaven given among men by which we must be saved" (RSV). Amen.

30
Sought and Found

J. C. WENGER

On Christmas Day, 1910, I was born in Honey Brook Township, Chester County, Pennsylvania, the son of A. Martin and Martha Rock Wenger. On my father's side I was descended of Wenger, Martin, Sensenig, Weaver, and various other Pennsylvania German Mennonite families of Swiss descent. My mother's father was a Scotch-Irish immigrant of about 1882, and her mother was Pennsylvania German. Both my parents and all grandparents were members of the Mennonite Church. I had a very happy childhood. My parents were devoted Christians and truly loved each other. We children felt secure. I was the oldest of five children, three sons and two daughters. As a boy I enjoyed the schools of Cambridge and Honey Brook. I fished and swam in the Brandywine Creek, and enjoyed especially being with my father and the other employees in the mill of J. K. Lewis, Honey Brook.

As to my childhood religious life, again I was a happy boy. My parents truly adorned Christianity. When we moved into the town of Honey Brook the fall of 1918, Father sold our horse and buggy and for a number of years I generally worshiped at the Methodist Sunday school and church. Occasionally my father would borrow a horse and buggy and we would drive to the Old Road Mennonite Church at White Horse. After the purchase of a Model T touring car in 1922 we attended the Old Road Church

---

J. C. Wenger is a Bible and theology teacher in Goshen College and its Biblical Seminary. He has written many books and articles.

regularly. There I learned to love and appreciate the preaching of such men of God as C. M. Brackbill, and especially of Bishop Abram Martin. I also remember Deacon Landis Hershey with fond appreciation. The church song leaders were Dr. John Hostetter and John Rohrer. Harry Reeser was Sunday-school superintendent. We often drove over the Welsh Mountain to the Churchtown Sunday school on Sunday afternoon.

In this period of my life I really lived in two worlds: a rather secular society of boys in Honey Brook, and a very happy spiritual environment at the Old Road Church on Sundays.

In August of 1923 our family removed about fifty miles to Bucks County, Pennsylvania, where my father became janitor of the Rockhill meetinghouse, and where I attended eighth grade at Biehn's school and later four years of high school at Sellersville. Now for the first time in my life I lived in the center of a strong Mennonite community. I must confess that I was somewhat shocked to find the Mennonite community not quite as perfect as I had pictured our church communities in my mind.

As to my religious development, I suppose my first twelve years could be called in some respects, "Years of Innocence." To be sure, I did many things which I knew were not right, but I had no particular fears about my shortcomings. I enjoyed life immensely, I had a feeling of security in our happy home, I enjoyed Sunday school and church life, I prayed a great deal, and had no fear of eternity or of the Second Coming of Christ. However, from about ten to thirteen there began to be increasingly a certain uneasiness as to my spiritual condition. And when a call from Christ to become His disciple came to me in the spring of 1924, it was a total surprise. Up to this point in my life I had regarded the Christian lives of my parents as practically perfect. I felt especially close to them, for I knew that they loved me and that they were truly children of God. I had no doubt about the reality of their Christian experience. I took my father in particular as my model in every area of life. Upon learning that he was fifteen when he became a Christian, I early made the decision that when I became fifteen I too would unite with the church.

But at the age of thirteen, as I was going over this matter

again in my mind, that I would accept Christ when I became fifteen, there suddenly came into my mind a question from outside myself with startling clarity, "Why not now?" Immediately I recognized this as a divine call to yield to Christ and become a Christian. To this day I have no doubt about the reality of that interpretation, and immediately I made the decision that I would take Christ as my Saviour and Lord.

The real struggle was not the decision to accept Christ. The real struggle was to make that decision known to my parents. I decided to postpone any announcement until evening. But the supper hour came and passed without my having mustered sufficient courage to make my decision known. Finally, as I was preparing for bed I said to my parents with considerable feeling, but as casually as I felt able to do so, "I guess tomorrow I will tell Alfred that I am going to join church." (Alfred A. Detweiler was the minister in the Rockhill congregation.) My father seemed deeply moved and replied, "We are very glad to hear that." That night he followed me to my room, and after I was in bed spoke to me of the great significance of the decision which I had made, and knelt by my bed in prayer for my spiritual welfare.

At this point I think I was happy with the beginning of my Christian life. During the following weeks, however, I came to be rather deeply troubled. I had supposed that when a person became a Christian his soul would be flooded with joy, so that he could always cuddle that happy "saved feeling" and stand on the ground of his feeling as a child of God. Because I was so extremely introspective as to the adequacy of my Christian experience, I actually failed to realize the sense of joy and peace which could have been mine, had I learned immediately to put my eyes on Christ rather than on my "experience." In any case the problem of assurance was intensely real to me. I lacked assurance, and yet I was too timid to report this to my parents or to the ministers of the church.

The other mistake which I made was the assumption that now that I had decided to be a Christian, the major battles were over. To my dismay I discovered that the major battles were just beginning. These battles involved the usual temptations of youth, particularly in the areas of holiness and tranquillity. I was possessed of a terrific temper, which was easily aroused and which really blazed. Through my tempestuous teens my father was especially kind and understanding. He put much confidence in me, treated me as a man, gave me enormous liberty to express my personality, and was deeply concerned that I should learn to master my temper. His greatest contribution came when one day, at a time I was not angry, he spoke kindly and gently to me of the tragedy of a person growing up without learning to master his temper. "What kind of man do you want to grow up to be?" he asked me. This appeal struck deep into my heart and was the means of my taking major steps forward and claiming more victory in Christ in this area of life.

Following my graduation from Sellersville high school in 1928 I had to stay out of school for a year because of the severity of the economic depression. From 1929 to 1931 I was a student at Eastern Mennonite School through the generosity of President A. D. Wenger, who took me into his home and gave me room and board at a ridiculously low figure. I was stimulated by many good teachers at Eastern Mennonite College. I mention particularly D. Ralph Hostetter, Chester K. Lehman, Ernest G. Gehman, and Daniel W. Lehman.

Following my graduation from junior college in 1931 I again lost a year, as far as further education was concerned, and entered Goshen College as a junior in 1932. Here I enjoyed my science courses under such men as Glen R. Miller, S. W. Witmer, and Paul Bender, also my Bible courses under such professors as H. S. Bender and G. H. Enss. The fall of 1934 I entered Westminster Seminary near Philadelphia, where I was stimulated by such professors as Machen, Kuiper, Murray, Woolley, Allis, Stonehouse, and MacRae.

At this period in my life, when I was twenty-five years of age, I began to court a Mennonite nurse of my home congregation, Ruth D. Detweiler, who had been born in West Rockhill Township, Bucks County. We were united in marriage on April 3, 1937, and God has graciously blessed our home with four children, two sons and two daughters.

After two years in Westminster Seminary, I enrolled at the

University of Zürich in Switzerland, where I studied under such scholars as Brunner, Gut, Köhler, Kümmel, and Zimmerli, and at the University of Basel, under Professors Barth, Köberle, and Eichrodt. I earned the Doctor of Theology degree at the University of Zürich in 1938.

The fall of 1938 I began to teach at Goshen College and its Bible school, which is now known as the Biblical Seminary. I also attended several summers at the University of Michigan, Ann Arbor, where I secured the Master of Arts degree in philosophy, 1942.

I have greatly enjoyed my teaching at Goshen College. It has been my aim to perpetuate the Anabaptist vision, to lead students to an evangelical faith in Christ, and to promote a Bible-centered faith. I believe profoundly in the understandings which our spiritual fathers, the Anabaptists, emphasized: (1) the church as a brotherhood; (2) Christianity as discipleship; and (3) the ethic of love and nonresistance. I hope that God has, in some measure, been able to use me in deepening the conviction in these matters of the young people who study at Goshen. The same concerns have motivated me in the various books which I have felt led to write. It is my concern that as a church we might be evangelical Christians, emphasizing the same truths which are the central emphases of the New Testament: conversion and the new birth through faith in a crucified, resurrected, and ascended Lord and Saviour, Jesus Christ; holiness of heart and life which takes away from people the desire to live in the sins of a worldly society; and a Christian life which emphasizes Bible study, prayer, church attendance, personal witnessing, and responsible stewardship. I am particularly concerned that our Seminary should graduate young men and women of God who know and love the Lord Jesus Christ, who accept the full authority of His Word, and who hold to the essentials of the "Anabaptist Vision" with simplicity of heart and devotion of soul.

I was ordained as a Mennonite deacon in 1943, as a preacher in 1944, and as a bishop in 1951. In all my church work I have earnestly sought to promote spiritual renewal and depth of Christian life and experience. I think that God has, in some measure, made clear to me that all religion without Christ, no matter how earnest, is of no value at all before God, that only in Christ is there salvation, forgiveness, eternal life, and spiritual healing. I have therefore tried to emphasize nonconformity to the world and spiritual separation unto God, a personal faith union with the Lord Jesus Christ, strict obedience to the New Testament, a major emphasis on missions and evangelism, and an earnest effort to be such transformed persons that love and nonresistance may express the true desires of our hearts.

It is my deepest desire to realize the place of service, and the effectiveness in it, which Christ has envisioned for me. I want to be a kind, considerate, loving, and loyal husband to my wife, who is my dearest and closest friend on earth. I desire to be a gracious and understanding father to our four children. I hope to become a more effective teacher of God's Word in all its Christocentric and ecclesiocentric glory. And finally I want to be a faithful servant of Christ in His church, in whatever appointments He gives me. I have tried to put my ministry first in my life. With all the strength which God gives me I have sought to help the Mennonite Church discover and perpetuate its unique heritage and mission, and to make that heritage known in Christendom.

As to my own character, I can testify to the reality of the insights of both Christ and Paul on the depravity of the flesh. I have experienced, with much suffering, the way the flesh resists the Spirit of Christ. My struggles have not been confined to personal holiness or to the control of my temper. Self-will, self-centeredness, pride—all these are a terrible reality. Yet I do desire in my innermost heart to be fully conformed to Christ in thought, motive, word, and deed. Left to my own resources I cannot even desire these qualities from an unselfish motive. As to the flesh I am therefore a wretched man. Yet I must always record my confidence in the Gospel, that Christ has died for my sins, "even mine," as John Wesley wrote. Hence I take my place joyously as wholly unworthy of divine sonship, knowing full well that I can be saved only by grace, divine and infinite grace.

I am particularly impressed by the objective significance and the relevance of prayer. I marvel again and again at the glorious way in which God through Christ hears and answers prayer.

It is my prayer that God Almighty may be pleased through Christ to keep me, weak as I am in myself, unto a happy end in Christ. It is my prayer that God may so fill me with His love and His peace that I may be a more acceptable instrument in His service. It is my confidence that by His measureless grace, the grace by which He called me, He may also preserve me, His unworthy son, unto a happy end in glory.

Yes, I met God. I met Him on a childish level in my preconversion years. I met Him on a deeper level at the master commitment which I made at the age of thirteen. And in the deepest sense He continues to reveal Himself to me. I did not seek Him, but He sought and found me. May His love transform me ever more perfectly into the image of His beloved Son.

31
The Bible Was Nonsense to Me

YORIFUMI YAGUCHI

I was born in a Buddhist family. My grandfather was a Buddhist priest and a bishop. He was well known in his district. It was believed that he had done some miracles. He could heal those who were sick mentally as well as physically, it was believed. During the war, he was most popular. People believed that if he prayed, their sons or husbands would never be killed in the war. Therefore many came to him and asked him to pray. He was once a missionary to Hokkaido, where our Mennonite missionaries have been working.

My father was not a Buddhist monk, but he wanted to be one. He was working in a local government. His role was to find out those young men who could fight well in the war. He was also a faithful believer in an emperor-god. He was extremely nationalistic. Thus I was brought up in a Buddhistic and Shintoistic environment.

I still remember that I walked with my grandfather, who had been visiting his members' houses and praying for them. Those members offered him a certain amount of money and rice, which I carried in a bag. He was highly respected and loved by them. He had a beautiful voice in reading the Buddhist scripture and in praying. I learned some while I was with him.

My father told me that the emperor of Japan was a living god.

Yorifumi Yaguchi is a Japanese Christian, a member of the Mennonite Church. This testimony was written while he was a student at Goshen College Biblical Seminary, Goshen, Indiana.

We should worship him, and we should even die for him, if he wants us to, he said. Japan is a divine country. She has never been defeated and will never be, he said. He also taught us how to pray to Shinto gods and how we should pray to Hotoke. Any man becomes Hotoke, a sort of god, after his death, we are told. In our house we had two Hotokes, my younger brother's and my younger sister's. We used to pray every morning. We first offered them a small amount of rice in a cup and soup, and then we prayed. We prayed that we might spend the day safely. We prayed that we might pass the examination. We also prayed that Japan might win the war. We loved the Shinto gods. Their stories were a sort of lullaby to us.

Naturally, I wanted to be a Buddhist, and moreover, at a certain time of my youth, to be a Buddhist monk. I had a strong desire to retire from the transientness of this world. I would sit in my grandfather's temple for hours to meditate. It is at the foot of the mountain, and there I was not bothered by anyone. Sitting in it, I tried many times to kill all my earthly desires and tried to be one with nature. I wanted to feel the impulse which is believed to be working in nature. I heard that, if we practiced, it was possible for us to be conscious of the fall of one leaf from a tree a hundred miles away. And I tried. I wanted to achieve the Enlightenment.

After I finished high school, I entered college. It happened to be a Christian college. I was not interested in Christianity. I had been told that Christianity was a Western religion. Buddhism and Shintoism are traditional Japanese religions, and so, Japanese should believe in either of them or both of them, I thought. Tunes of Christian hymns were strange to me. They were sort of sweet, but they were Western nevertheless. Why should Japanese sing such songs? We have our own songs! The Bible teachers were most dry! Why should they press us Japanese to adopt Western customs? We students quite often discussed Christianity with each other.

"Hey, do you believe Christ was the Son of God?"

"By no means!" I used to say. "There is no creator God. You know Christianity is a fiction. The Bible is a fiction. You see, there are many contradictions in it."

"What are they?"

"Well, God is love, they say. But this God kills men, doesn't He? He also allows people to kill other people. How can He be love? The Bible also says that Jesus was born of a virgin. How could it be possible? How could they know that He was born of a virgin? But suppose He was born of a virgin, what does it mean? You know Gautama, the founder of Buddhism, was born of the virgin Maya four hundred years before the birth of Christ! Did Jesus heal many sick persons? Okay, there have been many Buddhist monks who healed sick men...

"The Bible is nonsense to me," I would say. "I couldn't understand it at all. Peter's mother-in-law caught cold. Jesus ordered the demon to get out of her. Then she became all right. What does it mean? The cause of this sickness is the work of the demon? What nonsense!

"Christians say, 'Love your neighbors and love your enemies,' but do they really love them? Atomic bombs in Hiroshima and Nagasaki are the expressions of it? Why don't Christians protest against the testings of H-bombs? Why do American Christians hate Russians so much? Why do Christians in the southern part of the United States hate Negroes? Love their enemies? Never!

"Missionaries! Okay, they can be the expressions of love. But how could we understand the fact that they live in a big, nice house? They have maids. They have cars. They dress well. They eat good things. And look at these people in Asia! They are in real poverty!"

I studied Christianity at school for four years, but I couldn't understand it. There were too many stumbling blocks to me, as there still are to many Japanese non-Christians. I thought the religion which could save the world from destruction was Buddhism, which teaches against killing.

I graduated from college, and then I became a teacher in a senior high school in Hokkaido, the northern island of Japan. I was at that time living in a Buddhist temple. It happened that a monk of that temple knew I was from a Christian college, and he supposed that I was a Christian. He tried hard to discuss religion with me. And then a strange thing happened to me. He talked ill of Christianity, and I began to protect it from his ill words.

One day, suddenly, the revelation came to me. I realized that I was not living a good life. My life had been distorted! Many sinful events in the past tortured me. I was a terrible sinner, I realized. This terrible consciousness of sin crushed all at once all my pride and purpose of life. Something was gravely wrong with me. I had been walking in a completely wrong direction! I was desperate. I feared. All hopes were gone.

I needed something. I needed gods to rely upon. I needed the love of Buddha so that my sins might be forgiven. But all these gods of Shintoism and Hotoke of Buddhism were nothing to me. They couldn't help me. They had no power. They were not living. They were not real. They were false gods. And at this moment words gushed out of my mouth: "O Jesus, forgive me and save me. I committed awful sins against you." I could realize that He was the Son of God, who died for my sins. I could know that He is living and has been working on me.

After that I was guided and helped by one of the Mennonite missionaries, and finally became a member of the Mennonite Church. Now I firmly believe that God wants me to serve Him through this church, and I thank Him for His love and guidance.

32
Saved to Sing

WALTER E. YODER

I was born in Lagrange County, near Howe, Indiana, on the Pretty Prairie, on January 8, 1889. This small prairie is a beautiful farming community and must have appealed to the early settlers as a good place to live and rear their families. A small Amish Mennonite church was started in this community soon after the Civil War. However, by the time I came on the scene the little fellowship was beginning to break up and families were moving out. My maternal grandfather, Jacob Hooley, moved from Wayne County, Ohio, to Lagrange County, Indiana, in 1864 and located near the Townline Church. After a few years he moved with his family to the Pretty Prairie. At the time of my birth he had sold his farm and moved to Cass County, Missouri. My uncle, Jacob Yoder, and his father-in-law, Christian Warye, sold their farms and moved to Johnson County, Iowa, about the year 1884. When I was three years old, my parents sold their farm and bought a farm on the Haw Patch in the southwestern corner of Lagrange County near the village of Topeka, Indiana. This community was known as a good farming community, and this may have been one reason for locating here. But I am sure that the principal reason for selecting the Haw Patch was that there was a strong, growing Mennonite church there.

Maple Grove had two young ministers who had been ordained

Walter E. Yoder served long as head of the Music Department of Goshen College. He is now living in retirement in Goshen, Indiana.

just a few years before. J. S. Hartzler, a young schoolmaster, was ordained in 1881, and Jonathan Kurtz in 1882. This church was also known for its strong Sunday school, and since there were seven children in our family when we moved here, this was also a strong asset. Some of the early Sunday schools in the Mennonite churches taught the German language, but as far back as I can remember, we were taught the Bible. The hymnbook of my childhood in the Maple Grove Church was *Gospel Hymns* Numbers One to Six. My mother was an excellent singer, and one of the happy memories of my childhood was singing Gospel songs as we drove the four miles to church.

The farm at our new home was an ideal place for children to grow up in close contact with nature. We had a small maple grove near the homestead where each spring we had the pleasure of seeing the trees tapped, and we helped gather the sugar water, and saw it evaporated and boiled down to maple syrup. Sure, we would have an evening with friends, and we would be treated to maple taffy and maple sugar. At the back end of the farm was a thirty-acre tract of virgin timber. Through this timber ground there was an open ditch with running water the year round. It emptied into the Emma Creek in the far corner of the woods. What a fine place to cool one's feet on a hot summer day and to hunt crayfish, or to lie on top of the gate across the creek and fish for "shiners" with a string, a bent pin for a hook, and a fish worm, a bug, or a grasshopper for bait. And what a joy in the spring and early summer to wander among the large trees and shrubs, wild flowers, trilliums, the jack-in-the-pulpit, and May flowers. Or, after harvest to go back to the southeast corner where we had a small swamp and find the bushes of huckleberries. In the autumn the big woods had walnuts and hazel nuts. What joy! This was a child's paradise.

My first three years of school were in a one-room country school with its eight grades. After my oldest sister was ready for high school, my parents decided to send all of us to school in Topeka. Here the first six grades were in two rooms and the junior high school had two grades in one room. This led naturally into the high school, since the high school was in the same building.

I graduated from high school in 1908. The following summer I went to Goshen College for preparatory work for teachers. I taught a seven-month term in Lagrange County and returned to Goshen College in time for the spring twelve-week term, and remained for the summer session also. Thus, one year after my highschool training, I had taught a term of school and picked up a year of college normal credit. This was followed by my second year of teaching in Lagrange County, Indiana, after which I decided to go back to Goshen College and take a music teacher's course. At the close of the 1910 summer session I went with J. J. Fisher to his home in Johnson County, Iowa, taught a fall term of public school, and taught my first singing class at the same time at the East Union Church, Kalona, Iowa.

One of my early Sunday-school teachers was Bertha Zook, who later married I. R. Detweiler. They were two of our early missionaries to India. I was a young boy thirteen years old when our bishop laid his hands on their heads and commissioned them to go forth with the Gospel of Jesus Christ. I was greatly impressed with the scene of our church sending out its first foreign missionaries. After several years of service in India it was found that Mrs. Detweiler's health could not bear the rigors of missionary work in India, and they were forced to return home. This also impressed me because of the way God overrules in the lives of His children.

It was a part of the regular program of the Maple Grove Church to have a series of evangelistic meetings every winter. In December of 1903 our evangelist was Jacob S. Gerig, Smithville, Ohio. I was in the eighth grade of school, and as the meetings continued my heart became a battleground. Christ through my conscience was speaking to my heart telling me that I was a sinner and in need of Him as my Saviour. The devil was saying that I was too young and should wait a few more years. Then one evening as I was endeavoring to slip out with my burden, a good brother named Melvin Lantz stopped me and said, "Walter, we hope you will accept Christ. I am praying for you." This personal touch, I think, was what I needed, but that night and all the next day the battle raged in my soul. When I returned home from school and was helping with the chores, I finally said, "Lord

Jesus, I accept you as my Saviour; tonight I will make a public confession."

Immediately peace flooded my soul. How real and how precious that experience has been through all these years! I must confess that there were a few times when the cares of this world and neglect in my devotional life dimmed the glow of this first experience, and I had to ask with Cowper, "Where is the blessedness I knew when first I saw the Lord?" This has happened only with my neglect; Christ has always been near when I returned and confessed my sin and neglect. It has been almost sixty years since that first experience with the Lord, and He has grown more precious to me as the years rolled by.

Another experience that has been with me and acted as a governor through all my life happened at one of our Indiana-Michigan Sunday-school conferences about the time I was a junior or senior in high school. The conference was held in a large tent in the maple grove across the highway from the old Maple Grove Church. Sometime during the conference M. S. Steiner, president of the Mission Board, came on the ground. He came with a definite purpose to present the cause of missions to the conference. During the last evening he preached the closing message, presenting the cause of Christ in a powerful way, calling upon young people especially to commit their lives fully to Christ. I stood at his invitation, indicating that I would be willing to serve Christ when and where He might lead. This pledge has ever been before me in every major decision of my life.

I must now go back and pick up another thread that influenced my entire life. I must have been about ten years old when late one summer afternoon a Mr. Roscoe from the Wilson Music Company in Goshen drove into our yard with a one-horse spring wagon in which he had a beautiful reed organ. He asked my parents if they would permit him to leave this instrument in our home on trial. He would be back in a few days and pick it up again if they did not wish to buy it. There was no regulation in the Maple Grove Church prohibiting families from owning an organ, although very few families had such an instrument. My parents and all the children enjoyed music, and all could sing, as we often did in our home. We children huddled around our parents to hear what the decision would be.

Since it was late afternoon, my parents invited Mr. Roscoe to put up his horse and stay for the night. That evening we played the organ and the family stood around the organ and sang from the *Gospel Hymns*. We had many hymns memorized and we could sing in four-part harmony, as Mr. Roscoe added the beauty of the organ tone. What a joyful evening that turned out to be! You guessed it. The organ was bought, and soon after I began to take lessons. My teacher taught me more of the music fundamentals than organ technique. I learned to play all the scales and all the keys, both major and minor. Then she followed with the arpeggios of the tonic, subdominant, and dominant chords in all the keys, both major and minor. This knowledge was a great help to me when I later began my study of music theory in college.

After teaching public school two years in Indiana, and after my first singing class in Iowa, I felt that my life would be in some phase of church music, and I was determined to go on with my music studies. John D. Brunk had set up a music curriculum at Goshen College in 1906, and was head of the department when I began my music education. He was a fine Christian gentleman, an excellent teacher, and a man who had at heart a desire to develop and train the Mennonite Church in the best tradition and style of unaccompanied congregational singing. I owe much to this fine teacher for the interest he instilled into my life for good hymn singing and an improvement in our church hymnody. It was he who taught me that we were in danger of losing our heritage of good hymns because of the demand in the church for the more subjective Gospel songs. I finished the music teacher's certificate course in 1913.

During the school year 1912-13 at Goshen College William B. Weaver was chairman of the extension department of the Young People's Christian Association. He was eager to see the college send out a Gospel team. After looking around for a place to serve, he contacted Harvey Friesner, minister in the Barker Street Church near Mottville, Michigan. Brother Friesner accepted the idea of having a Gospel team come to his church for ten days of evangelistic effort. The college gave its permission, and a team was organized with William B. Weaver, chairman, A. W. Geigley, minister, and W. E. Yoder, song leader. O. O. Miller was to be prepared to give special talks to young people and children; and Aaron Eby, fifth member, was head usher and in charge of personal work. We formed a quartet with Miller and Eby tenors, and Yoder and Geigley bass. The meetings began on Friday evening with only about a dozen people present including the team. This was discouraging and called for special prayer, seeking God's will and guidance. The second evening found a few more hungry souls in the audience, which encouraged us to continue, and by Sunday evening the church was well filled.

What a hungry audience that was, how they drank in the Word, and enjoyed the quartet, and the singing of the congregation! We were all thrilled when a few evenings later there were those who stood and accepted Christ. On Thursday evening about a dozen accepted Christ as Saviour and Lord, and when the meetings closed, twenty persons had found Christ. After the meetings were over Brother Friesner asked William B. Weaver and me to continue coming to Barker Street and to help to consolidate the work, assisting those who accepted Christ to decide on a church home. We continued to go to Barker Street until the close of the school year in June. About a dozen of those who accepted Christ joined the fellowship at Barker Street. There is no fuller joy in all our Christian life and experience than that which is found in bringing others to accept Christ as Saviour and Lord.

The winter of 1913-14 A. W. Geigley and I conducted meetings in the Mennonite churches of Indiana, Ontario, and Ohio, our final meeting being at the Youngstown, Ohio, Mission, where Mr. and Mrs. T. K. Hershey were in charge of the work. Other ministers with whom I worked during the next few years were S. E. Allgyer, C. F. Derstine, J. S. Hartzler, and C. Z. Yoder. Working with these fine ministers in evangelistic meetings was one of the richest spiritual experiences of my life.

Now we come to a fifteen-year detour. Two important events of my life happened in the year 1917. First was our country's entrance into World War I in the spring of 1917. I was caught in the military draft. I claimed exemption on the grounds of my religious conviction that war was wrong and that it could not be supported by a Christian. The plans I had made with the churches in North Dakota, Saskatchewan, Alberta, and Oregon for singing classes beginning in the spring of 1918 now had to be changed, because I could not leave the United States on account of the draft. I therefore canceled all those engagements and had to think of something else to do.

The second important event of 1917 was my marriage to Matilda Schertz of Metamora, Illinois, that autumn. My father-in-law, Peter Schertz, informed me that he needed a farmer, and since I needed work, I began to farm. My call from the draft board for my physical examination did not come until March, 1918. Since my farming operations were already begun, I informed the draft board of this and they placed me in class C-2, which excused me until after the 1918 crop was gathered. On November 11, 1918, the Armistice was signed by the German government, and the war was ended. However, now that I was farming I felt that God had somehow guided me in this direction and that I should be content and do what I could in the Metamora Mennonite Church and community. There was much good talent in the church that I felt needed encouragement and use. Most of the time during those years I had some music projects going so that the young people were getting practice in reading music and singing in the various services of the church. In 1935 the men's chorus was organized with members from Metamora, Roanoke, and Calvary Mennonite churches. We rehearsed one evening each week and gave many programs in many different churches. Six children came into our family during these fifteen years.

I came to Goshen College in 1930 to direct the music at the young people's institute. It was at this time that Dean Noah Oyer asked if I would consider coming to Goshen to teach music and to direct the choruses. I told him that I was hardly prepared for that, but he encouraged me by saying that I could continue my studies after I began my teaching. I told him that I would have to think and pray about this and take up the matter with my wife.

This was, indeed, a difficult problem for us to decide. J. D.

Brunk had died in 1926, and the Board of Education was not in favor of a strong music education program. Some members of the board were at that time opposed to teaching any instrumental music, and with this program I could not agree. The music program at the college had been floundering for a number of years, although I thought that B. F. Hartzler was getting it under control and was doing very commendable work with the choruses. We finally decided that Goshen might be the place that God wanted me to serve, and I accepted Dean Oyer's invitation to come to Goshen as teacher of music. President S. C. Yoder visited us some time later and arrangements were made for my work to begin in September of 1931. I continued my education by attending summer sessions at Northwestern University until 1937, and received my Master of Music degree in 1938.

The first four or five years we were at Goshen College were very difficult for all concerned—the students, the faculty, and the administration, as well as the constituency. Money was scarce, farm prices were hitting the bottom, many banks closed, and the country was groping for a way out. Many times we had to ask ourselves and God, "Have we made a mistake?" When our faith sometimes seemed to waver, and the road ahead looked dark, and we were about to say we had better go back to the farm, then I would look to President S. C. Yoder, who had a much more difficult task than I, and new hope and faith would spring up in my heart so that we would decide to go on for another year. It was during those hard years we decided to stay by this task and see it through with the other members of the faculty. These were great years at Goshen College, when students and faculty knew each other intimately and God's blessings were abundant.

In 1941 our country was again engaged in a World War. This brought about a drought of young men in college. We would hardly have had enough men for the A Cappella Chorus if it had not been for the men in the Seminary who were glad for chorus experience. But at the close of the war the students began flocking to the colleges, and Goshen's attendance grew by leaps. The college was soon in need of more buildings. During my years in the music department the following buildings were erected: the Library, Union, Westlawn women's residence, High Park women's residence, the Arts building, and the Church-chapel. With more students, more faculty help was needed; Mary Oyer joined the music faculty in 1945, and Dwight Weldy in 1949. I continued to teach until the close of the 1956-57 school year. The twenty-five years at Goshen College were good years for me as I look back at all that happened there. Goshen College has found new life, new services, and a wholesome vigor as a younger faculty have come in to carry on the work some of us have laid down.

I was elected as a member of the General Conference Music Committee the summer of 1913. At this meeting General Conference commissioned the Music Committee to prepare a book of Gospel songs for use in mission stations, young people's Bible meetings, and evangelistic meetings. In the spring of 1914 the committee met in the home of C. Z. Yoder, ex-chairman, near Smithville, Ohio, remaining in session for almost a full week. Here we compiled the songs for *Life Songs,* published in 1915. It was while working on *Life Songs* that the committee became aware of the weakness of many songs for instilling a deep worship experience. It became a common occurrence during this committee meeting to have S. F. Coffman or J. D. Brunk call a halt, and begin a speech which usually ended by showing the need of the Mennonite Church for a standard hymnal for her church services. This resulted in a recommendation to the General Conference for such a hymnal. In 1919 General Conference commissioned the Music Committee to begin gathering material for a church hymnal. The Mennonite Publishing House helped the committee by purchasing hymnals of other denominations and encouraging the committee in its work. We had full committee meetings one week each year until the work was completed in 1927. I was co-opted as a member of the committee when they met at Goshen College in the summer of 1937 to compile *Life Songs No. 2,* which was published the next year.

For a number of years I was on the summer Bible school staff of the College congregation. It was at this time that I saw the need for four-part harmony songs for the juniors. I made some arrangements for our use in the Bible school, and then kept on making more arrangements until I had many songs. At our next annual meeting I presented these for criticism and evaluation. The committee agreed with me that our church needed such a book of songs for our junior meetings. It was agreed that we should ask the Publishing House to publish this collection of junior hymns. The Publishing House saw the possibility of correlating songs for juniors with the summer Bible school courses being prepared at that time. There were some forty songs suggested by the people writing the Bible studies which were sent to me for arranging and adding to the song collection. Thus *Junior Hymns* was born. I have helped in the compilation of all the songbooks published by Scottdale since 1913. The two newest books were *Songs of the Church,* published in 1953, which was conceived as a book for church choruses or as the book to replace *Life Songs No. 2. Our Hymns of Praise,* a songbook for children, is a songbook for children from preschool age to sixth grade. We are now working on a revision of our *Church Hymnal.*

I am continually thankful to the Lord for health and strength to be able to work on this important project which may have much influence in shaping the hymn worship materials for the coming generation.

I can say with the psalmist:

> Bless the Lord, O my soul:
> And all that is within me,
> > Bless his holy name.

> Bless the Lord, O my soul,
> > And forget not all his benefits:
> Who forgiveth all thine iniquities;
> > Who healeth all thy diseases;
> Who redeemeth thy life from destruction;
> Who crowneth thee with lovingkindness and tender mercies;
> > Who satisfieth thy mouth with good things;
> > So that thy youth is renewed like the eagle's.

33
Forty Years at MPH

ELLROSE D. ZOOK

For some reason I can find no record of the day, month, or year when God through Christ became a reality in my experience. But of all childhood experiences, my meeting God stands out vividly. The time is of little significance; the experience was true and unimaginably rewarding.

As a young boy of about twelve I cannot remember of any heinous sins that I had committed beyond those a growing boy normally falls victim to. So far as I can remember there was very little "sin" to confess. Of course there were the little lies, bad-tempered moments, and disobedient acts.

Although the cloak of whatever self-righteousness I might have been wearing needed to come off for a cloak of the righteousness of Christ, this theological viewpoint was of little concern to my young mind. I don't think I ever arrived at a point where I was consciously aware of self-righteousness. There was no moralistic goodness that stood in the way of accepting the call of the Holy Spirit in answer to the prayers of parents, ministers, and teachers.

Thus today in retrospect it becomes clearer. The invitation from Christ was not so much away from heinous sin and immorality as it was toward Christ as a Saviour and lifelong Friend and Companion. It was an invitation to come to the One who loved and cared for the young and almost innocent. It was an invitation

---

Ellrose D. Zook, originally of Allensville, Pennsylvania, is Executive Editor, Mennonite Publishing House. He and his wife, the former Frances Adeline Loucks, live in Scottdale, Pennsylvania. They have twin sons, Mervin and Merlin.

to a friendship that would be living, safeguarding, and guiding through the years to come. For that night as I stepped out of the side door of the little white frame church after Christ met me, I looked into the starry sky which in its beauty confirmed forever in my soul that I had found a true and eternal Friend.

But this was only the beginning. From here on perhaps it may be more truthful to say that God met me in various calls to service and witness for Him. There were testing experiences in high-school days. After each mistake God in some way reminded me of the error and the need for confession. Some of the real testing experiences came in times of working on various jobs away from the farm. How a person is kept in the center of God's hand in these experiences is a mystery, or perhaps one should say a miracle of faith which parents and ministers have in God for youth.

Leaving home at the age of seventeen for a short term of service at the Altoona Mission brought some new experiences. A short time later, in January, 1925, God led me to the Mennonite Publishing House. Here was an opportunity to serve the church as well as to find a vocation. Here God met me time and again through such persons as Aaron Loucks, J. A. and Lina Z. Ressler, John L. Horst, C. F. Yake, Levi Mumaw, A. J. Metzler, Ben Gamber, Henry Hernley, and others.

At this writing it is almost forty years since I began service in the publishing interests of the church. During this period there have been intervals for education and farm service during World War II. In the early years at Scottdale the vocational choice eventually had to be made. Here I am deeply indebted to a friend and fellow worker, John L. Horst, for his counsel that no better place to be of service to the church could be found than where I was at the time. The counsel was wise and true.

But testing time was on its way. It soon became evident that in a "Christian" institution there were people with all the human weaknesses of people in other walks of life. The idea that an institution engaged in church work would have workers with no problems and no conflicts was soon to be shattered. It was the daily devotional worship periods of the workers that proved to be a place where God had time to speak to us through His Word.

Somehow through prayer, fellowship, and worship we all gained strength to go on in the face of difficult situations.

It soon became clear that there was really no such thing as a "Christian institution," but only Christian people working together in service for Christ. These people all had different degrees of spiritual experience and understanding, partly because of the many backgrounds and communities from which they came. There were no halos on the workers, much less on the product of the institution that went out to the churches. In my own mind I finally was led to see that the product of this institution which I served reflected the spiritual insights and quality of the persons who produced it. All the religious printed material that went out did not serve to put halos on the workers; neither could the workers put halos on the materials just because they were religious.

There was still a deeper testing time to come. In all my experience in printing, editing, and writing, God eventually made it clear that there was no salvation in any operation, whether of machines, materials, ideas, or people. Any activity was sacred and successful only as it was a work of faith in Christ and the church. Blessing and fruitfulness came only in the service of faith and not in any kind of physical or intellectual exercise.

Finally, the greatest testing came in human relationships. After all, which was more important, the worker or the work? A delicate balance between the two seemed to be God's answer. Both were important. Neither could be fully sacrificed for the sole benefit of the other. Both were subject to the will of the church. I remember well some of the difficult times in the institution's history. They were times that tested severely one's loyalty to Christ and the church; but God spoke through these, too.

During these past years one must wonder why he did certain things and why he didn't do other things. It all began with a simple "yes" to the evangelist who invited me into the kingdom of Christ. But that was a babe in Christ speaking only the simple words that a child can speak. Today the words are, "Yes, I believe; I follow; I serve." But God met me in all these personal relationships, service activities, and worship experiences rather than I meeting God.